**Also available from the
Keys to Mental Health Series**

8 Keys to Mental Health Series

Babette Rothschild, Series Editor

The 8 Keys series of books provides consumers with brief, inexpensive, and high-quality self-help books on a variety of topics in mental health. Each volume is written by an expert in the field, someone who is capable of presenting evidence-based information in a concise and clear way. These books stand out by offering consumers cutting-edge, relevant theory in easily digestible portions, written in an accessible style. The tone is respectful of the reader and the messages are immediately applicable. Filled with exercises and practical strategies, these books empower readers to help themselves.

8 KEYS TO PRACTICING MINDFULNESS

MANUELA MISCHKE REEDS

FOREWORD BY BABETTE ROTHSCHILD

W. W. Norton & Company
New York • London

The Three-Part Breathing and Breathing with the Earth in Mind mindfulness exercises are adapted from Reginald A. Ray (Touching Enlightenment. Findings Realization in the Body), pages 367–372, 361–366. Use with permission by SoundsTrue.

The Heart Practice exercise is adapted from Reginald A. Ray. Used with permission by Reginald A. Ray.

For information about permission to reproduce selections from this book, write to Permissions, W. W. Norton & Company, Inc., 500 Fifth Avenue, New York, NY 10110

For information about special discounts for bulk purchases, please contact W. W. Norton Special Sales at specialsales@wwnorton.com or 800-233-4830

Manufacturing by RRD

ISBN: 978-0-393-70795-3 (pbk.)

W. W. Norton & Company, Inc., 500 Fifth Avenue, New York, N.Y. 10110
www.wwnorton.com
W. W. Norton & Company Ltd., Castle House, 75/76 Wells Street,
London W1T 3QT

1 2 3 4 5 6 7 8 9 0

For Kirian and Tristan

Contents

Acknowledgments

A book project like this is a labor of love. From writing it to receiving input and testing the ideas on students and clients, I have been part of an interconnected chain of aware people who care greatly how we live in our bodies and minds.

I am grateful to Babette Rothschild for being a visionary in the field of body-mind psychology and giving me this incredible opportunity. Thank you to Deborah Malmud for supporting this project. A very special thanks to Stephanie Baker, whom I truly could have not done without. Her feedback and keen editor's eye have been invaluable. A special thanks to my husband, Michael Mischke Reeds, for his advice and kind words of encouragement. Many thanks to Betsy Burdock and John Perrin for feedback and cheer-leading. Thank you to Marylyn Genovese for her research help. A heartfelt thanks to all my amazing clients and loyal students, who have inspired me with their quest for an embodied life; thank you for letting me test the many exercises in this book. A big thank-you to my sons, Kirian and Tristan, who let their mom write even when it wasn't fun to be without her. Because they take mindfulness for granted already, I know there is hope for the next generation to live embodied and emotionally balanced lives. A deep bow to Monika Mischke-Renner, my first and most impactful teacher of compassion and kindness. Deep gratitude to my meditation teachers at Naropa University for inspiring and guiding me as a young student in the teachings of Chögyam Trungpa. Finally, a special thank-you to Reggie Ray, my meditation teacher. You have inspired me to trust my heart and body—not just with words but with your fierce compassion.

Foreword

Babette Rothschild, Series Editor

Mindfulness can be helpful in such a variety of circumstances that it was important to include a book focusing on everyday mindfulness in the *8 Keys to Mental Health* series. Being mindful can help you to make decisions, assess circumstances, calm yourself in stressful circumstances, and so on. Mindfulness is a way of feeling connected yourself and your surroundings, regardless of what is going on. When we are mindful, we are in the here and now, fully present.

Mindfulness—as you will see in these pages—is not the same thing as meditation.

Mindfulness is a practice of being aware in the present moment, which anyone can do at any time. Being aware of your gut as you decide whether to order the Caesar salad or the hot fudge sundae is an application of mindfulness. Taking a break during a stressful argument to feel your feet, be aware of your breath, and clear your head, is an application of mindfulness. Pausing to feel the emotional impact of an upsetting email and reflect before responding is also an act of mindfulness. Though many religions utilize mindfulness as part of their practices, being mindful need have nothing to do with religion; it can be (and often is) purely a secular activity.

The practice of mindfulness has experienced a resurgence in recent times. Though select populations have been practicing mindfulness and meditation for several thousand years, it is a commonly mistaken belief that it is a new discipline, particularly when connected to self-help and psychotherapy. Mindfulness has actually been woven into psychotherapy and body psychotherapy for nearly a century. Gestalt therapy, best known via Fritz Perls, one of its founders, has mindfulness as a major feature. Those familiar with Gestalt will recognize the foundational "now I am aware" exercises as being rooted in present moment mindfulness. In addition, many types of body psychotherapy have utilized the mindfulness aspect of body awareness as a base. Other methods, including Core Process that originated in the United Kingdom in the 1990s and Hakomi Therapy developed in the United States in the 1980s, have always woven mindfulness and meditation in to their disciplines. In fact, author Manuela Mischke Reeds is a therapist and trainer of the Hakomi method. It is one of the reasons she is a particularly good choice to author this book, *8 Keys to Mindfulness*.

The modern-day resurgence of mindfulness into the field and practice of psychotherapy also has its roots in the popularity of at least two publications: Jon Kabat-Zinn's *Mindfulness Based Stress Reduction* and Marsha Linehan's *Dialectical Behavior Therapy* both of which first appeared in the 1990s. Influenced by these innovators, in the last couple of decades, mindfulness instruction has often been sought by those in physiological or psychological distress and integrated into physical as well as psychotherapy healing programs and disciplines.

One of the most important factors for utilizing everyday mindfulness is the recognition that you do not have to meditate to do it. In fact, though meditation is a practice based in mindfulness, they are two separate things. Of course, regular meditation practice will enhance one's skill in mindfulness, but it is not a prerequisite.

This book highlights the importance of an individualized approach to Mindfulness practices that advocate for everyone to "do it" the same way, is a kind of oxymoron. How can I be mindful if I am doing it like everyone else? Throughout this volume, Mishke Reeds invites you to "try this" and explore what suits and what does not. This type of evaluation of finding what works particularly for you is one of the most important foundations of mindfulness.

In these pages you will find "everyday mindfulness tips" that will help you apply what you are learning, further tailoring what is best for you. Throughout you will be reminded that mindfulness is a choice that makes many other choices possible, including containment, calm, and compassion.

I approached Manuela Mishke Reeds to write this book for the 8 Keys Series because I knew her to be adept at applying mindfulness to mental health. She has long practiced mindfulness for her own benefit as well for that of her clients. You will find her stories and instructions to be full of warmth and solid knowledge, guiding you to find the tools that are most helpful in promoting your own mental and physical health.

Introduction

This book is about learning how to pay attention to the present moment. It draws upon body-based mindfulness practices that I have learned as a longtime meditator and somatic psychotherapist as well as an international teacher of psychology and meditation for over twenty-five years. If you strive to be more awake and alive in your daily life; if you feel stressed, want to improve your relationships, or gain more resources to get you through hard times; then the 8 Keys in this book will help you foster the calm, sustained, and more mindful inner state that leads to rejuvenation, connection, and confidence. Although the 8 Keys may be particularly helpful for people who suffer from stress, they will also be useful for anyone who wants to live in an embodied way by meditating and practicing mindfulness.

I took on this project because I want to help people learn positive approaches for working with their particular challenges. In fact, the idea for this book was driven by the requests of my clients and students, who kept asking me to write down the meditations I was teaching them. My clients are of all ages and present a wide range of issues, such as stress, trauma, anxiety, depression, and addiction. My students come from all over the world, and many of them are health practitioners, psychotherapists, physicians, and consultants who want to use mindfulness in their line of work. Both groups wanted a way to take what they were learning out of the therapy office or classroom and into their lives so they could improve their emotional balance and better themselves on a daily basis.

Mindfulness can be defined as the ability to be present with your experience without judgment. It is the capacity to witness your thoughts, feelings, and sensations with curiosity during both ordinary moments and dramatic ones. Recall the times when you felt attentive to what was happening inside or around you. Perhaps you were skiing down a powdery mountain on a clear, cold day, and you could feel your body being completely in sync with each turn or bump on the trail. Perhaps, when you became a parent for the first time, you held your newborn infant, and in that moment you were content to look into her sweet face without needing anything else. Maybe you remember a challenging circumstance, such as the illness or injury of a family member, when you were jolted into realizing what is important to you.

When you are mindful, you are aware of the here and now, fully present with what is. In this book I will guide you again and again to this quality of presence. When you are not present, you are constrained by qualities such as fear and anticipation. Being present means you can see, feel, and sense what is truly happening on a continuum that can range from feeling gratitude for your life to observing painful moments or patterns. Over time, by being present, you will be better able to focus on what works and what you want to change. You will actually be able to see what is good about yourself and others and make decisions based on this state of wakefulness. Of course, "getting" to this state of mind means you begin with whatever is happening *right now*. At times, this is not easy to do. Obstacles may arise that can challenge you at your very core. The good news is that you can apply the 8 Keys right now.

The 8 Keys will be introduced through stories and descriptions, and you will learn to apply the teachings by doing the exercises. There are also mindfulness tips along the way that you might be inspired to try. As you progress through the chapters, you will also find inspiration from recent research about mindfulness and its health benefits. Contemporary neuroscience provides a powerful understanding of how the brain works, including how emotions and behavior are impacted by meditation. Since my training and teaching have been in the contemplative psychotherapy realm, I draw extensively from what I have learned in the field with my clients and students. Please note: Although psychotherapy can be a helpful tool, it is not a requirement for becoming mindful. The universal need for contemplation is reflected in many cultures and traditions, including the Buddhist, Christian, Jewish, and Islamic religions. However, the exercises here are nonreligious and accessible to anyone regardless of background.

Keys 1, 2, and 3 help you slow down and establish a basic practice by providing guidelines for posture and breathing. Once slowed down, you can learn about the disposition of your mind toward a more natural state of calmness. Keys 4, 5, and 6 address the challenging terrain you will likely encounter and how you can work with it as you practice. This includes identifying obstacles, working with feelings and sensations, and learning how the body is a resource. Keys 7 and 8 invite you to deepen your practice by sustaining calmness and choosing an abundance way of thinking rather than a scarcity state of mind. This may, in turn, inspire you toward compassion and kindness.

This book delivers you to the doorstep of your mind and body, where you will gain a deeper awareness of the body-mind resources you already possess. I will help you to identify pitfalls and entice you with facts from research, but learning to be mindful means making time to practice and striving to enter a more mindful way of being. With the 8 Keys, you will find guidelines for making the most of the practices as well as various options for meditations that involve sitting, walking, gently moving, or lying down. You can try these exercises at your lunch break, before you rise, or before you fall asleep. But best of all is for you to sprinkle mindfulness throughout your day. There are many opportunities to apply mindful practice: talking to coworkers, taking care of an elderly parent, being a leader in the community, teaching children, or simply dealing with the stressors of everyday living. I can guide you and teach you how to address the challenges, but you will have to listen to yourself. Practicing mindfulness is about discovering what works for you and trusting your experience.

If you are new to the idea of mindfulness, take your time and absorb the 8 Keys in sequence. The first three chapters build a foundation that is important to learn in the beginning stages of practice. Slowing down, assuming the correct posture, and paying attention to your breath and body are steps that are tempting to skip, but I recommend that you learn the proper setup. As a beginner, it is easy to make the assumption that it isn't necessary to learn how to sit with the right posture or that you don't need to practice at all. You might think that mindfulness is already there in everything you do, but there is a crucial difference between making an intention to be mindful or thinking you are mindful and *practicing* mindfulness. The formality of sitting down and making time to practice is the training ground. Becoming more mindful in how you eat, conduct your relationships, or do your work is the fruit of your formal practice time.

When you slow down and become conscious that "I *am* being mindful," you will likely discover unexpected or surprising details in your life, environment, or body. You might notice a feeling of sadness or joy you haven't been in touch with before. Or you might notice sensations in your body like warmth, lightness, or relaxation in your chest or belly. You might observe how you are going over the same argument in your head or how you haven't let go of an old way of thinking. The purpose of becoming more mindful in your life is to become more attuned to how you feel so you can make conscious decisions to change. This may mean becoming gentler with yourself. For example, if you have challenges with food, you might pay attention to what kind of critical voices go with that. Maybe there is an opportunity to be kinder to yourself when making the next food choice.

If you are a seasoned meditator or are already familiar with mindfulness, you might look for a new angle or deeper understanding on how to become more mindful by using the body in your practice. Although this book is aimed as an introduction, the awareness that comes from mindfulness practice is multilayered. Each time you engage your life mindfully, you uncover new opportunities to learn more about yourself. I recommend that you pay special attention to the body-based exercises in this book. They can provide deep experiences that will take your understanding in a new direction. If you have already felt the benefits of mindfulness in your life, you understand the value of practice. In the exercises, experiment with what you have already learned and deepen your understanding. The challenge for anyone who has prior knowledge of a topic is letting go of what is known and being open to new possibilities. If you can appreciate what you have already gained and reenter the arena with an open attitude, this will serve you well.

Whether or not you are new to these practices, working with mindfulness has several facets: First, you need to understand how you are organized internally. For example, do you get annoyed when people talk about their feelings? What does that mean to you? You could say you just don't like it when people get sentimental or warm and fuzzy. You could also look at what this discomfort indicates. Of course, you might still prefer not to share your feelings with others, but how you respond in your next encounter might be different. Another aspect of working with mindfulness is identifying what you want to change and looking for opportunities to implement small shifts. Imagine an area of your life, such as your relationships at work. Maybe you face a situation where you don't feel appreciated or remain unseen by your colleagues or supervisors. As you proceed through the 8 Keys, you may gain some insights into how you can initiate small yet promising changes.

Practicing mindfulness can also lead you to recognize what is going well in your life. Focusing on slowing down or appreciating the relationships you have can be deeply satisfying. Keep in mind that without actually trying the 8 Keys, you will not gain the insights that come from experiencing something new or seeing a familiar problem through a different lens. All of us need both insight and practice—they go hand in hand. In other words, we need to actually *experience* change in order to *create* lasting change. Current brain research teaches that the brain is constantly changing through novel experiences, both positive and negative. Fortunately, this can go both ways. Stress and trauma leave a mark on our body and brain, but we can also create positive changes by cultivating mindfulness and body awareness. In addition, focusing on what works well helps us call on the resources we already have to address the challenges in our lives. In this book, I will guide you toward awareness that can help you find your strength in the face of adversity.

Various characters are introduced throughout the book to illustrate common problems and how mindfulness practice helped them. You will meet a mother striving to be an effective parent, a harried and driven executive, and a young veteran struggling to live a normal life. This book was inspired by witnessing the powerful ways in which mindfulness has transformed the lives of my clients and students. A common complaint I hear from both groups is that they are tired of being stuck in their heads and want to learn how to be in their bodies. Through the use of these exercises, many people have successfully incorporated mindfulness into their daily lives and rediscovered how to connect to their bodies. As you read, you will find that these people are smart. They have figured things out, and so can you. What they all have in common is the desire to become calmer, happier, and more fulfilled people. They want to know what has real meaning in their lives. Please note: I have used many of their stories to illustrate a variety of applications; however, identities have been changed to protect privacy and confidentiality.

As you embark on this journey, keep in mind that practicing mindfulness is not about being better by figuring it all out. It is about learning to be more curious about the struggle and tolerating the moments when you don't know. In the process, you may learn to become a more balanced and holistic person, someone who has the emotional capacity to learn and grow from adverse situations, to muster kindness in the face of hardship, and to show compassion even if it doesn't result in immediate reward. When you are mindful, you feel, sense, intuit, and think. You become a more generous human being who fulfills your potential by making choices with both your heart and your intellect. You learn to trust your experience. It is this trust that grows over time and allows you to become your own wisest friend and counsel.

Introducing Everyday Mindfulness

Becoming mindful is about the small, everyday things, such as pausing to take a breath before you drive off in a hurry or considering for a second the food that will nourish your body before digging into a meal. Or it can mean checking in with yourself before responding to a challenging email or text. Every moment of our lives can become an opportunity to practice mindfulness. In this book, I will invite you to sharpen your awareness and ask yourself more frequently, *What do I notice right now?* or *How do I need to respond or be with this situation?* You can then observe your boredom, contentment, frustration, or calmness without having to react. These seemingly tiny moments of noticing yourself can have a major impact on your life as you learn to track habitual patterns and awaken to more presence. Moment by moment, you have the opportunity to cultivate the awareness in your everyday life that will make a difference in how you engage in your activities and relationships.

Explanation of Exercise Icons
and Levels of Practice

There are three levels of practice. Begin with the first level by setting the right frame. Second, treat the exercises as an experiment in staying with and studying what happens. At the third level, anchor your experience by noting, writing about, or contemplating what has happened. Take an extra moment here to harvest and hang out; don't just jump up and move on. These three levels are described in more detail in the first chapter.

Three Levels of Practice

1. Set the right frame
2. Stay and study
3. Anchor and harvest

Exercise Icons

Watch for these icons. They indicate the recommended meditation posture. The minutes following the icon are a recommended minimum time for the exercise.

Mindfulness Practice Positions

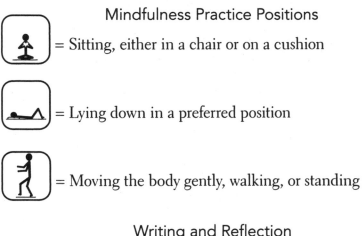

= Sitting, either in a chair or on a cushion

= Lying down in a preferred position

= Moving the body gently, walking, or standing

Writing and Reflection

= Writing and reflecting on the experience of the exercise to uncover or integrate your meditation exercises. This will help you to better understand what you're dealing with.

8 KEYS TO PRACTICING MINDFULNESS

KEY 1

MEET THE PRESENT MOMENT

Your true home is in the here and the now.　　　—Thich Nhat Hanh

Young children have a remarkable capacity to be absorbed in the details of a moment with curiosity and wonder and without self-awareness or criticism. They may spend long minutes examining the shape of a bug's antennae, marveling at the color of a butterfly's wing, or tracing the pattern of raindrops dripping down a windowpane. They possess an intense curiosity for whatever is happening this very second, without judgment. As an adult, you are fully capable of being as open and aware as a child. Yet you may easily forget that you have this ability. The culprit may be speed, worry, anxiety, laziness, emotional patterns, bad habits, or stress. In any case, the simple experience of being present gets lost, and you spend your time anticipating what will be or lamenting what has been. Your daily life is driven by cycles of hope and fear. You dwell in the past or future, but not the present.

Mindfulness can be thought of as a way of being open to what is within and around you. The word *mindfulness* is the English translation of the ancient Pali word *sati*, which means awareness and remembering (Bodhi, 2000). Like a curious child, you can look at what surrounds you with no preconceived notions, just an open engagement with whatever is happening now. Although you are an adult, you can remember that this possibility is available to you at any moment.

Most of us need time to connect, to be social and engaged, but we also need time to reflect and retreat. The ebb and flow of engagement and withdrawal is an ancient need of our mammalian bodies and reflects the natural rhythms of our biological system. We move toward excitement to join, belong, and be stimulated. Then we retreat to quiet spaces to lick wounds, heal, reflect, or savor what has happened. We can become sick, disturbed, or disconnected from our own inner wisdom when we don't make the time and space to slow down and find inner peace and balance. Often, when we are in a hurry, we make choices based on efficiency, comfort, or the need for safety. Mindfulness is actually a part of our natural way of being and a way to help us rebalance. When we can access it as a tool, it becomes an inner compass, directing us toward health and sanity.

Mindfulness Versus Meditation

Most people associate meditation with images of a statue of the Buddha or someone praying in a church, synagogue, mosque, or temple. Being mindful is different from meditation. When mindfulness is engaged systematically, we call it meditation. You gain more mindfulness when you practice this way. In this book, the exercises are meditations, but think of them as training wheels for becoming a more mindful person. When you aren't engaged in formal meditation, you can practice mindfulness by stopping to wonder at something beautiful or notice a moment of sadness. These moments of awareness are the benefits of formal practice. You gain the ability to shift into a different awareness because you see yourself as you are experiencing emotions and sensations. Formal meditations, such as the exercises in this book, help you fuel and recharge so you can sustain a more balanced emotional life.

Although mindfulness has its roots in Buddhism and other spiritual traditions and has been practiced for twenty-five hundred years, it is not a religion. It is not something you need to sign up for, join, or even agree with. It's an ability you already possess. As humans, we have the capacity to self-witness, to be aware, to tune in and find out for ourselves what we are feeling, sensing, and needing. I often hear students ask if they need to become Buddhist to be mindful. No, you do not. There are many cultures and traditions that place self-reflection or quietude at the center of a fulfilled spiritual life and value reflecting and listening to one's heart. Our modern culture rarely helps us cultivate mindfulness, but mindfulness has recently been recognized by the medical establishment as well as popular culture for its many benefits.

Overall Benefits

You can expect to receive four overall benefits from practicing mindfulness, each of which builds upon and enhances the others.

1. Calmness
2. Creativity
3. Effectiveness
4. Connection

To begin with, being calm is essential. Without it, you fall prey to the speediness of your mind and actions. You may make mistakes or decisions you later regret. When you are in a calm state, your creativity arises naturally, although you might not think so at first! Remember a time when you went on a long drive or worked on a project without any time constraints. You might have had innovative ideas for remodeling your kitchen or implementing something new at work. This space of calm actually enabled your creativity and playfulness to come forth. You can't be fully creative if you don't have some room to discover a new thought or new insight.

There is evidence that increasing playfulness enhances productivity, lowers stress responses, and creates an overall sense of happiness. Forward-thinking companies are recognizing the value of creative play and mindfulness for their workers. Google, Apple, and Yahoo, for example, offer meditation classes to their employees to help them minimize stress as well as increase their ability to focus and pay attention (Capurso, Fabbro, & Crescentini, 2013; Jha & van Vugt, 2011; Lutz, Slagter, Dunne, & Davidson, 2008).

When you are playful and calm, you are more effective at your work. By taking mini-breaks and interrupting the routine, you get to enjoy what is happening in the moment. Recent studies (Jha, Krompinger, & Baime, 2007; Jha & van Vugt, 2011) show evidence that regular mindfulness training stabilizes emotions and trains attention to be more stable and focused. A stressed body and mind can shut down and become focused only on survival. As a human being, you do not thrive by shutting down but by feeling safe, supported, and connected. You are more productive when you experience calm and spaciousness, and your full creativity can arise only in the absence of stress and worry.

A calm and spacious mind considers other people by noticing that there is a need and demonstrating generosity and compassion toward that need. Reaching out to others is more than just something nice to do. Brain studies show that we are neurologically wired to connect with others. The research on infant attachment (Schore & Bradshaw, 2006; Siegel 2013) has shown us that we thrive on connection and become more caring and considerate when we are considered by others. Babies who are not lovingly cared for can have trouble attaching appropriately to a caregiver and therefore not learn innately that they are loved. This feeling of being loved translates directly to how we love the world around us. To be considerate of others, we need to care about ourselves and know ourselves; otherwise, we have nothing to give. Think of mindfulness as a kind of mental and physical technology to give you more room to sense, feel, and innovate.

Health Benefits

There are many direct health benefits for people who practice mindfulness on a regular basis. Many studies have shown emotional, physical, and psychological improvements. Highlighted here are the most commonly cited and important studies, demonstrating (1) relief from stress and pain, (2) improved memory and brain function, and (3) an enhanced capacity for emotional regulation as well as empathy. Throughout the 8 Keys, I will examine each of these three groupings in more detail. Many exciting studies reveal the direct mental and physical health benefits to our body and mind from mindfulness practice, and we will not only read about them but consider their impact. Here are a few highlights:

Reduced Stress/Anxiety symptoms
Several studies have demonstrated that, after six to eight weeks of daily mindfulness practice, symptoms of stress decrease dramatically. Results have shown less anxiety, improved sleep, and an increased ability to handle stressors and improvement of overall wellbeing. (Bruckstein, 1999; Hölzel 2011, Kabat-Zinn et al, 1992,).

Improvement in PTSD Symptoms
An estimated two hundred thousand veterans suffer from PTSD symptoms (U.S. Department of Veterans Affairs, n.d.). In one study, (King, 2013) eight weeks of mindfulness treatment yielded 73-percent improvement in symptoms. Promising studies are under way to understand the effects of mindfulness meditation on PTSD veterans. The emphasis on nonjudgment, focus on attention, acceptance of emotions, and awareness of self-blame help PTSD survivors decrease their symptoms (Follette, 2009; King, 2013).

Reduction in Chronic Pain
In a chronic pain study, subjects reported that after four days of mindfulness practice, they experienced 40 percent less pain (Zeidan et al., 2011).

Assistance in Combating Addiction
A key element in combating addictions is the ability to acknowledge the underlying reactivity without activating addictive behavior patterns. Studies have demonstrated improvement in the ability to quit smoking (Davis, Fleming, Bonus, & Baker,

2007) and reduce illicit substance and alcohol abuse (Bowen et al., 2006) in subjects who practiced nonreactivity and equanimity in meditation. The impulse to act out, or exhibit self-destructive behavior, was lessened, and the ability to self-soothe improved (K. W. Brown, Ryan, & Creswell, 2007).

Better Heart Health
After five days of meditation (compared to relaxation techniques), meditators in one study showed improvement in their heart and respiratory rates (Tanga et al., 2009).

Improved Memory and Attention
In a famous Vipassana meditation study (Lazar et al., 2005), meditators showed improvement in memory function and overall brain health. Gray matter in the right anterior insula, left inferior temporal gyrus, and right hippocampus—regions of the brain responsible for body awareness—was more concentrated in those who practiced meditation, allowing the practitioners to experience more body presence and sensations. These structural changes in the brain resulted in increased attention regulation and somatosensory processing.

In a study, on brain changes of long-term meditation practitioners brain shrinkage was less over time than those of nonpractitioners. The implication being that the aging prefrontal cortex thinning process is delayed. As the meditators' cortical brains retained thickness (a phenomenon called *gyrification*), their working memory increased (Lazar et al., 2005).

In yet another study, mindfulness meditation increased practitioners' capacity to "observe and accept" by improved their attention and regulation as well as their executive functioning (Jha et al., 2007).

Better Emotion Regulation
Meditation increases output of the hormones serotonin and dopamine, resulting in pleasant and euphoric feelings. This ability to "be with" strong emotions and decrease reactivity results in better emotional regulation. When you are more bal-

anced emotionally, you are not as easily triggered (Desbordes, 2012).

In a mindfulness study, participants showed more acceptance and less avoidance of their feelings and unwanted thoughts (Bowen, Witkiewitz, Dillworth, & Marlatt, 2007). The use of regular mindfulness yielded less emotional distress and more positive mind states as well as self-reported overall better quality of life (Toneatto & Nguyen, 2007).

More Compassion

One of the most important benefits of regular mindfulness practice is an increase in empathy, kindness, and self-compassion. When the body and mind are calm, the emotions become regulated and self-compassion arises. This affects not only the individual but also his or her immediate relationships.

Three studies have shown this change. In an eight-week study on mindful self-compassion, participants demonstrated a lessening of feelings of isolation and self-judgment and more ability to relate to painful experiences (Germer & Neff, 2013).

In another study, nurses showed more compassion toward their patients after mindfulness practice (Beddoe, 2004). In a study of parents of disabled children, the mindful parents showed more capacity to handle challenges and their children displayed an increase in positive behavior (Singh et al., 2006). In general, caring compassionately for others has further benefits and is associated with increases in overall well-being, self-compassion, and self-esteem (Baer, Lykins, & Peters, 2012; Breines & Chen, 2013).

Lifetime Benefits

You may still be asking, *Why do I want to be mindful? What does it give me? I am already present in my life and in my actions.* At the same time, you might also be considering whether you are happy or living the life you would like to. If you are interested in creating a life that is more meaningful, mindfulness might be a way to do so. Think of mindfulness as a skill set to help you answer or address these questions. A Harvard study found that we spend 47 percent of our waking hours wandering in our thinking mind. When we wander, we are not in the present moment, and this decreases our overall happiness (Killingsworth, 2013).

If you want to make changes in your life, practicing mindfulness can be relevant right away. You can become present in any life activity. For example, if you want to change your eating habits, start slowing down during the process of preparing and consuming food. If you find yourself dissatisfied in an intimate relationship, try putting some effort into listening to your partner. When you want to have a better quality of life, give yourself a "tech break" and leave the mobile phone or tablet at home while you take a walk and carefully observe the details of your surroundings. Get curious about what happens when you find yourself in these familiar "stuck" places. Like everyone else, you have to start from where you are in the moment. Changes that come with being mindful are incremental and cumulative. You may not notice changes because you are in the moment and experiencing them, yet they are happening as you pause and observe.

To begin, ask yourself, *What do I want to do differently in my life?* Once you know what you want to work on, there are many applications for bringing mindfulness to this intention. This book offers the training and tools you need to work on any area in your life you want to improve. Becoming mindful is about waking up to what is not satisfying and taking a new approach by catching yourself in habitual responses and tuning in. If you find yourself in the same old struggle with your teenager, see if you can wait and watch for your reaction or response before firing back. If you get aggressive while driving, try observing when you tailgate the car in front of you. Tell yourself you would like to drive more defensively next time. If you find yourself hurrying to every appointment, envision what it would take to arrive 5 or 10 minutes early and how good it might feel not to rush. You can become a mindful parent, a mindful driver, a mindful lover. The key is making some time for the "cushion"—that is, the exercises in this book, which are the "rehearsals" necessary for bringing mindfulness into your everyday life. When this "sitting time" gets translated into daily living, you will reap the benefits. Of course, becoming mindful doesn't mean you won't have negative feelings or experiences, but you will become better equipped to handle life's challenges.

If you find yourself struggling with the inevitable demands, stresses, or emergencies of life, such as aging, illness, caretaking, loneliness, or fear of death, mindfulness can ease your suffering by offering a way for the mind and body to inquire into itself and create new emotional pathways. We all suffer, no matter our circumstances or age, and we don't have a way around the facts of life, but we can have a way of being *with* suffering that directs us toward healing, understanding, and compassion. By becoming mindful, we have an opportunity to understand and clearly see the *causes* of our suffering and how the past is influencing the present.

My clients often say, "I don't want to dig up the old stories. I've done that. It's just too painful." The truth is, the stories of the past still dominate the present despite our best attempts to move on or bury them. Unconscious habits and addictions are the vehicles by which the past still works on us. But during mindfulness practice, we meet the past *in the present* and gently dismantle its power. It's like updating an old file. The more you arrive in the present, the less the past has a chance to repeat itself. The troubling events of the past become faded memories and eventually loosen their grip over your body and emotions.

How to Get the Most From This Book: Guidelines and Foundations

Each chapter will have exercises along with stories and explanations to help inspire and guide you in a regular mindfulness practice. To reap the benefits of mindfulness, it's imperative to practice, so consider these guidelines and foundations to be a way to support and ground your efforts.

Guidelines

Guideline 1: Find a Safe Place

When you do the exercises, find a quiet, undisturbed space where you can retreat for the time you will be practicing. Choose a spot that is pleasing to you. Some people like to set up a special or inviting space with a cushion, a flower, or a candle. For others, finding a place to practice means simply closing the office door or sitting in the car to create a moment of privacy.

Guideline 2: Listen to Your Body

Most exercises are done sitting down. You may sit on a chair or on the floor using a meditation cushion. You may also lie down. (I describe posture in more detail under Key 2.) Take care of your body and adjust to your needs. Some exercises include lying in a comfortable position, walking, or moving slowly. Experiment with finding a balance between alertness and relaxation. Follow the pleasure principle: If an exercise doesn't feel right, don't do it, or modify it to suit your needs. This doesn't mean there won't be some discomfort at times, but the general guideline is to trust your inherent wisdom and whatever comes up. I recommend trying the exercises with your eyes closed because it will enhance your ability to "be with" your inner experience. Some people, however, are more comfortable having their eyes open. That is fine. Discover what works for you.

Guideline 3: Practice, Practice, Practice

I have provided suggestions for length of time, but consider taking at least 10 to 15 minutes per exercise. These exercises are for your own discovery and can be repeated many times. In fact, I recommend doing them several times, as their effects will deepen with practice. Our brain is organized to recognize repeated patterns. The more you practice, the more you will benefit as you let go of the "not knowing" anxiety you may carry and relax into your experience. If you can carve out 15 to 30 minutes, wonderful! Make the time you have work for you. It's okay to start slowly and build up.

The more you make this a habit and give it your time and effort, the more you will gain.

These exercises are designed to help you think, reflect, and begin a mindfulness practice, and in this process, you are sure to learn a lot about yourself. However, if you find that the exercises are bringing up emotional issues that need more facilitation, please consider consulting a treatment professional or psychotherapist. If you have persistent depression, anxiety that does not settle, or disturbing memories, please seek professional help.

Foundations for a Successful Practice

Foundation 1: Set the Right Frame

Often we go into an exercise halfheartedly and then are surprised if it doesn't seem to change anything. The way we approach an exercise has everything to do with the outcome. Decide on an intention or focus before you begin. This can be as simple as saying to yourself, *I am taking this time now for myself. I am making space for this exercise. I would like this to teach me.* In this way, you are showing yourself some respect for what you will do next. This intention honors the experience and the result. You can also apply this concept to your everyday life. Before you begin any activity, you can set the right frame, which can help you focus and make the best of new learning experiences. The intention you set can be as simple as *I would like to settle my body, I would like to be more attuned to my kids right now, I am slowing down to feel what is happening right now,* or *I would like to enjoy this evening with my friends.* Extend the benefits of the exercise and make mindfulness work for you in your life by making these intentions applicable to right now and any situation you are in.

Foundation 2: Stay and Study

Allow yourself to stay with the exercise and study your experience without any judgment or agenda. This will open up possibilities for noticing something new—for example, a sensation in the chest you never felt before, a feeling of gratitude, a new thought, a clarity you never experienced before, a memory, feelings of sadness or peacefulness. Be curious about the situation. Stay with it. It means you are letting your attention be with the focus of your experience. You are actively disrupting the wandering of your mind. You come back to your body and breathe again and again. Then you study whatever is happening with an open attitude. This foundation is especially helpful when you encounter challenging emotions.

Here's an example of what it might look like to engage with this process. As you begin an exercise, you may notice all kinds of things, such as your wandering thoughts. Maybe you feel bored or distracted. Maybe you want to give up. But then you stick with it. After a bit, you may notice you feel a little more at ease. In your next conversation with your partner, you feel more in tune with him or her. Your thoughts have changed slightly; you are more patient. *Hmmm*, you think, *maybe I will try this exercise again.* Then you sit again, you try another one of the exercises, and it's a little easier. After a while you get tired; you even fall asleep. *Ah, what a failure*, you might say . . . and then you read that one of the obstacles is getting tired. *Okay*, you say to yourself. *That is okay.*

You decide to try again. Breathing, slowing down, you notice feelings and sensations. You notice a resistance to all this. *Why bother? But this book says that it's important to stay with it.* Again you stay with it. You breathe slowly, in and out. This time, you notice a little more spaciousness. Many thoughts arrive; elaborate stories wander through your head; you seem to come up with long to-do lists. *Yikes*, you think, *I did it wrong again.* You take a break.

You try again. You want to discover what this is about. *Okay*, you tell yourself, *the exercise is encouraging me to get curious. I'll try that.* Now you're learning that your mind does something interesting: It repeats the same pattern, scanning for to-do lists, going over arguments with your spouse, preparing for the work day, rehashing old stories, dreaming of escape. So much busy thinking. Will this ever end? You realize this is what you do: think and be busy and ruminate. You get suspicious that you're not being mindful at all.

You try again. This time there is a moment of no chattering in your brain. *So quiet . . . ah, delicious! . . . this is new. Cool, something different.* But then, the pesky thoughts return. You have to make a deadline, call the contractor, make dinner—on and on the thoughts spin. You know this now and decide to come back to your breath by simply breathing in and breathing out. You notice a sensation in your body; you realize that it feels good to stay with your experience and listen. You let it be there.

You stay and study and notice there is no story, just sensations and feelings moving through. A sense of calm, connected and quiet. This feels interesting. Then the commentary comes back, and you begin to analyze it. Every now and then you realize how the chattering is not so important or that there's a little pause between thoughts, and you catch yourself being here and now in the present moment. You notice that you are more relaxed and not as focused on the next big stress of your life. Your mind and perceptions are changing, and there is a sense of being more in tune with yourself and your life.

Foundation 3: Anchor and Harvest

After completing the exercise, review the experience you just had and repeat to yourself what you have done. What was important? Did you have a new feeling or insight? By repeating something you discovered, such as *I could feel sad and not be overwhelmed,* you anchor the experience. Repetition strengthens neuronal connections in the brain. As an early brain researcher stated, "What fires together, wires together" (Hebb, 1949). Because of this principle, you will better remember the experience if you make a conscious effort to do so. This is especially important when new sensations arise, as their meaning can easily be forgotten. Linger long enough so you can reap the benefits of what you have just done. Don't jump up too quickly from any exercise. Stay a little longer and notice what has changed. You are gaining and noticing the benefits. The work is done; there is no effort. Simply hang out with the satisfaction of having finished.

Remember when you last enjoyed a satisfying meal, and bring this memory into the present. After a hard day's work, you sit down to enjoy food and refreshment and the company of friends. You sit back, and the fullness of this moment is about being happy and content with all there is. It doesn't mean the troubles of your life are gone, but in this moment you linger in the gratitude of having friends, of tasting food, of feeling your body being nourished, of being alive. It's good and you can have this moment. I consider this an essential practice: When moments are good, full, or happy, mark them with your awareness. You can say to yourself, *This is a good and happy moment.* I tell my clients that these moments are like money in the bank for when things get tough.

Getting Started: Take Your Baseline

You will begin your mindfulness discovery by taking a baseline "measurement" of what is. A baseline is a reference point that lets you know where you're at before you begin a process. Engineers and chemists use the concept of a baseline to identify a starting point, which they compare to later results. My use of the word is to be taken literally: How are you feeling in your body in this moment? For example, you might start with becoming aware of the tension in your shoulders. Without realizing the stress of the day, you might feel hunched over or caved in. After the meditation, check back with where you started and see what has changed. Did the shoulder tension change? The idea behind a baseline is to see what is present now so you can study the effects of the exercises later on. Without a baseline, you won't have any evidence for comparison. It's easy to take for granted that you feel better, yet forget that when you started out, you were tense. It's important to collect your own evidence of what makes a difference in your health and well-being.

A primary goal in the mindfulness journey is to train your mind to be less preoccupied with thoughts and feelings and to become more open and spacious. This takes training and returning to the basics of awareness of breath and body again and again. A secondary goal is to track the insights you might gain from taking this baseline. Recognizing that you are tired and need sleep can be a simple realization yet very important to your health. Noticing that you are agitated and that you need to take a walk to blow off steam before meeting your ex-partner might be another insight gained from taking your baseline. Consider keeping a journal devoted to these observations.

Exercise: Taking Your Baseline

 *15–20 minutes + 10–15 minutes writing*

Important: You will need paper and pen for this exercise as well as a quiet, comfortable, and safe place to sit. Give yourself 20 to 30 minutes in this space. You will also want to set a timer so you don't have to keep checking the time.

1. Set the Right Frame

- Take a moment and settle down into a seated position on a chair or on a meditation cushion. Make sure your pen and paper are close by. Ideally, your eyes are closed, but go with what is comfortable for you.
- Set an intention for this exercise, such as *I want to be present* or *I am open to what is there*. First, pay attention to your body and get curious. Feel the way you sit: Is your spine curved, or upright and straight? Are your muscles tense or relaxed? Are you comfortable? See if you can just listen to your internal body experience without much expectation or judgment.

2. Stay and Study

- Observe your breath by placing your attention on its rhythm. Is it fast? Slow? Pay attention to where you feel the breath right now. In your upper chest? Belly?
- Notice something about the breath—perhaps a smoothness, or even a staccato quality.
- In this very moment, see if you can just be with yourself.

There is nothing you need to change. You are simply taking a baseline of what is.

- Stay with the experience you are having. See whether there are tensions in the body. See if your mind is racing with thoughts or images. You might become aware of feelings that are in the background. Just let them be.
- Become aware of what is happening for you right now, in this moment.
- Then get curious about these thoughts, images, feelings, and sensations.
- Touch into these moments of discovery and then let them go. To do so, focus on your breath again, specifically the out-breath. Let the thought go with that exhale.
- You might discover more thoughts. Let yourself return to your breath, exhaling and releasing any tension.
- Try not to judge your experience, but pay attention to what is happening. Stay with your attention. Be present to what is happening right now and be curious.

3. Anchor and Harvest
- After your timer goes off, linger for another moment.
- Remember back to the beginning of the exercise when you sat down and made your intentions.
- What is different now?
- If you noticed tension in the body, what has released?
- If you had lots of thoughts, images, or feelings, are they different now? Have they calmed?
- What is the overall climate in your body, breath, and mind right now?
- Sit in reflection as you transition to the next phase. You can either stop here or take another 10 minutes and write what has come up (see below).

Writing:
- Write for 10 to 15 minutes. You can use this time in many different ways: to reflect, to summarize, to inquire, or to go

deeper into a theme. You can either reflect on the experience you just had or look at what got in the way of sitting quietly. Were there any obstacles for you? Did you have some insights? Perhaps a message came through? Was there anything surprising? It is helpful to do this several days in a row or repeat this as you proceed through the 8 Keys.

- After you have finished writing, sit quietly for 1 to 2 minutes more and review what you wrote and felt during this exercise.

A Baseline Difference

One morning, after Gaby dropped off her teenage twins at their bus stop for school, she had some extra time on her hands and decided to visit her art studio to finish a project. She turned to leave as the bus began to pull away, but just then the mother of her daughters' friend drove up, and the girl slammed the car door and ran after the bus. The driver stopped and the girl disappeared into the open door. Gaby waved to the other mom, acknowledging the near miss. The mother walked over and with a flushed face spilled her morning story to Gaby. "If my ex-husband had taken better care of my daughter, he wouldn't have forgotten her violin last night. I'm so tired of covering for him." In an agitated tone she continued to share details about the divorce and the challenges of being a single parent. Gaby listened, aware that her free time was slipping away. Then abruptly the mother paused. "I'm sorry. Here I am telling you all about my morning and life drama, and I've not even said hi to you." They both smiled, pausing. In a flash, Gaby's rising impatience vanished. Instead, she felt warmth toward this mother. As Gaby walked back to her car, she realized that she had been a little grumpy and not at all as calm as she had assumed. She felt connected to this woman; a small moment of shared intimacy had made Gaby realize that she was not alone in being a parent.

In a seemingly unexceptional moment, this exchange opened up a small world inside Gaby. She hadn't realized how grumpy and alone she often felt as a parent. The feeling she acknowledged after this encounter made her aware of how challenged she felt raising teenagers. Her newfound appreciation of herself and the other mother lingered the entire day. Your baseline, like Gaby's, is never far away. It's right there in each moment, offering its insight, allowing you to get in touch with what matters.

The difference taking your baseline can make can be recognized in other caretaking situations, like being with an ill parent. In such circumstances, there often isn't much time for your own desires and dreams, and you might feel trapped having to take care of someone else 24/7. Imagine taking your baseline before you walk in to greet your dad. You sit quietly for 5 minutes, check in with your breath and body, and ready yourself for the task ahead. Your circumstances haven't changed—your dad still won't recognize you—but you might catch yourself being softer as you sit with the sadness or joy of being with him.

You can also see the difference taking your baseline can make when challenging situations arise at work. For instance, suppose you arrive one morning to an email from your boss explaining that he is not happy with the new person you hired. This reflects badly on your choices. You are about to get called in for a meeting. You are nervous. You wonder how this will reflect on you. You worry that you did something wrong, or that this will have negative consequences for your project. Here's another opportunity to take your baseline. You notice the tension in your neck. You realize you haven't eaten since this morning, and a little jitter goes through your body. You pause for a moment to register the effects of this anticipation. You don't have time do a complete exercise right now, but you can still utilize this moment of awareness and simply notice. *I am hungry, jittery; I am nervous.* With that awareness, you can make a shift. You get food, sit down, and take 15 minutes before the meeting to center yourself and take care of your body. You feel better—still nervous, but also more confident. You recall the decision you made when you hired the new person. You are able to defend your choice. This is another example of how stopping to notice can make a change in your everyday life.

Taking your baseline at seemingly insignificant moments in your life can have a lasting impact. For instance, a colleague of mine, who later became a dance therapist, was taken by surprise early in his career when he met his first mindfulness teacher. Like many athletes, he was more concerned about how well he was performing as a dancer and less focused on how his body felt from the inside. He was asked bluntly by the teacher what the experience of dancing was for him. He was taken aback because it seemed so obvious to him; he had been trained to perform, not to savor his experience. He was instructed to sit down and practice mindfulness. It helped that he was in Japan, a foreign country and out of his comfort zone. This allowed him to question and wake up to what was truly important. The teacher repeatedly asked him to get quiet, listen, and notice what was happening inside. In essence, he was being asked to take his baseline. He soon realized that he was highly trained, but not in touch with what he wanted in his life.

After that experience, he changed careers and dropped out of the university he was attending in England. He moved to the United States, began studying meditation and dance therapy, and started living a life he had never envisioned. He discovered an alignment between his outer and inner life that gave him the courage to create what he had yearned for but didn't realize he had always wanted. Again and again, he learned to take his baseline and listen to what was present. This tool proved to be very valuable in his life. He began to practice mindfulness daily.

Years later, still a mindfulness practitioner, my colleague became aware of an underlying medical condition that was threatening his health. In tandem with medical doctors, he made wise decisions about treatment and continued to thrive. The capacity to tune in to his body, become quiet, and listen to his own counsel had become a tool, a skill, and a trusted friend. When you integrate mindfulness into your life, it becomes a constant companion, and you develop the ability to notice what doesn't serve you or is destructive. You gain the strength to follow the path that is right for you.

Everyday Mindfulness Tip

Start the day with a dose of mindfulness. Before you jump out of bed and get into your routine, take a quick baseline. What is the state of your body and mind right now as you snuggle under the covers? How did you rest? Are you anticipating a full and busy day? See if you can wait another moment before you get up. Return to your body and breath, exhale gently, and drop back into your resting position. What kind of day would you like to have? Are you yearning for more calmness and control today? Do you want to be invigorated and prepare for an exciting event? Or maybe you are dreading what awaits you at your desk or at school. Whatever your particular circumstances, see if you can relax one more moment, center yourself by returning to the baseline of right now, and notice and release the anticipated thoughts and feelings. Afterward, ask yourself, *Do I feel or sense anything different from when I first woke?*

KEY 2

START WHERE YOU ARE

Start where you are. Use what you have. Do what you can.
—Arthur Ashe, tennis player

You can realize mindfulness in a single moment—while in the middle of cooking dinner, walking your dog, tucking your kids into bed, or sitting in a business meeting. Suddenly you notice your breath or your posture, how you are feeling, the tone in your voice, the expression of a child or colleague. You watch yourself noticing. The experience is fresh and new even though you have been there many times before. This awareness fundamentally changes your experience.

Many mindfulness teachers have said, "Start where you are." This is an important teaching, because when you start where you are, you are already becoming mindful by making peace with yourself in this moment. This is the first big hurdle. It's not about achieving anything, going anywhere, doing anything special, or setting up the right circumstances, but rather realizing that whatever you are dealing with can be observed. You can literally start anywhere, at any time.

Lori, a client of mine who had devoted two decades of her life to building a successful career as a corporate executive, decided to take up skiing again. Having skied as a teenager, she assumed it would be easy and envisioned strapping on her skis, enjoying the glorious sunshine and beautiful vistas, and coasting down the slopes. Well, she was very wrong. Her body forgot that she had ever worn skis, let alone used them to go down a mountain. It was as if she had never skied before. Afterward, she described to me how her mind had wrestled with old perceptions of who she had been twenty years before rather than meeting the self she was right now. In our sessions, we worked on reminders that she needed to start where she was in the present moment. Again and again. No matter what age.

When you start with where you are now, a whole landscape opens up that you may not have realized existed. On her next trip, Lori began to accept her current skiing level. She reported feeling more relaxed. Instead of fighting with the past, she was in the present, appreciating that her body was not fifteen anymore. She realized how much she had grown and aged. It wasn't about what she had lost but what she had gained these past twenty years.

Mindfulness is learning to be with yourself anywhere—to trust what you feel inside. Soon after her skiing experience, Lori told me about riding on an airplane and how she had to deal with delays due to overbooked flights. She had never thought that sitting at the airport waiting for a flight could be just fine. Ten years before she would have been anxious over the hours lost or felt annoyed by her fellow passengers, but now she spent the time breathing quietly and tuning up her mindfulness. By the time she got on the plane, she felt relaxed and friendly toward the person sitting next to her.

Mindfulness experiences can be brief or extended, and respecting your own pace is crucial. This will enable you to take what you're doing seriously and reap the benefits. Allow yourself to start where you are and find your own way with the stories, explanations, reflections, and exercises. You may gravitate to some more than others. You can't just read about mindfulness any more than you can expect to learn how to play music or throw a football by just reading about it. You need to engage with the experience in order to learn and grow. Expect that some of the exercises will be easy and some will be challenging. The point is to try them out, learn from them, and inquire. Don't give up. If you feel challenged, that's a good sign: It means the exercises are working and you are encountering new terrain. Only by exploring uncharted territory will you gain new insights.

The Inner Witness

Try noticing your experience. This is critical for developing your inner witness, which is the capacity to observe and be with what is. As humans, we are equipped with the ability to think about thinking using the prefrontal cortex of our brains. We can see, feel, and taste but also reflect on what our experiences mean in the context of our lives. We track what is happening, and from this self-witnessing we arrive at understanding ourselves in a more holistic way. One of the crucial aspects of self-witnessing is that we learn how to decrease our impatience or irritation and become less reactive. When we feel irritation arising, for example, we can also choose to witness that emotion, and make a choice (e.g., *Maybe this time I won't act it out?*). But first, we have to notice.

One day, while waiting in line at the museum coat check, I saw a woman in front of me in the queue. She was visibly irritated at the clerk for not finding her coat right away. The tension rose in the small room filled with waiting customers as she pursed her lips, pinning her eyes on the frazzled clerk. The tone of her voice sharpened. The clerk searched frantically as the woman drummed her fingers on her purse. Finally, the clerk found the coat and, with a grin, handed over the prized item. The woman snatched the coat and stormed away without a second glance.

In a revised scenario, the woman could have become aware of her own irritation, taken a breath, and allowed for some pause, or maybe a kind word to herself or the clerk.

As you engage your mindfulness practice, you will see how you begin to follow your own experience and develop self-awareness. Studies verify that the capacity for awareness increases with mindfulness (Kilpatrick et al., 2011). The idea is to develop an inner witness who has no judgment about your experience. It just is. Scientific research has indicated that when the inner witness is established, it increases the capacity for empathy and kindness. For example, in an empathy study, a group of medical students self-reported higher levels of empathy after eight weeks of mindfulness practice (Shapiro, Schwartz, & Bonner, 1998). In addition, therapists undergoing mindfulness training reported more empathy toward their clients (Aiken, 2006; Wang 2007). When you can be with your experiences with curiosity, you are building an inner tolerance for your impatience, irritation, or any other emotion.

Experiencing the inner witness is a combination of feeling, sensing, and thinking. This is what meditation practitioners call an embodied experience. You see clearly and arrive at an insight, and what seemed emotionally charged or challenging before is now clear. Direct action can usually follow. Practicing mindfulness actively cultivates this self-witnessing capacity: You learn how to avoid being trapped by habits and patterns and instead wake up to your own intelligent nature.

Stay With Your Curiosity

When you witness your inner states, you also learn about your judgments. At first, you may notice what you like or dislike, but then you also learn how much time you spend judging yourself and others. My client Brad was an intensely self-judging person. He didn't like himself and considered his life a complete failure. He was depressed most of the time and had a "gloom and doom" attitude about everything. In our work together, I noticed he referred to little children as "menaces" or "problems." As he began doing mindfulness exercises, all he could feel and sense was his intense judgment and hatred for himself. He didn't like any part of himself that was tender, soft, or vulnerable—this only reminded him of his own childish qualities. Mindfulness was no fun for him at first. Judgments turned into lengthy liturgies in his head, and he could only beat himself up. But he bravely stayed with the exercises, and I encouraged him to stay curious about everything he was experiencing. I asked him to even notice how he could become curious about these intensely judgmental voices inside. As he stayed with that curiosity, he noticed a shift. A warmth entered his chest. He described it as a "welling up of liquid." Tears surfaced. He was surprised by this. But he was also genuinely touched by what was happening. It was the first "break" he'd had from his relentless self-judging. Staying with this experience guided him right through into the natural state of his mind and body, a place of generosity and warmth. This had been waiting underneath all along, but painful experiences had shut him off from this resource.

When we can be curious about whatever our inner witness reports, even if it's a judgment, we can open to the essential qualities that lie beneath, including warmth, empathy, and love. As we learn to relax our judgment, the positive qualities have room to enter.

Start With the Basics: Posture

This section of the book provides mainly technical instruction regarding how to sit, lie, stand, walk, move, or breathe during meditation. Positioning your body and setting intentions impacts the experience you will have. Allow some time to learn this. It will set you up correctly and save you some back pain. Many years ago, when I began my own mindfulness practice, I skipped this part of the instructions and had the attitude: *What's the big deal? I sit every day. I don't need any lesson on how to sit on a pillow.* In fact, I once walked out of a meditation class, skipping this instruction, and later crept back in when everyone had already started. This allowed me to stay in my comfort zone and not challenge how I was approaching my own inner witness. Later, I remember one of my teachers saying, "You don't go into a holy place, such as a church or synagogue, walk up to the front, and slap a sandwich on the altar. You approach and offer whatever you have with care and respect." In the same way, a respectful attitude will set the frame for your experience. Think of your posture and your approach as a way to enter your own special inner place.

Try this:
- Collapse your body, curve your spine outward, sink your chest, and drop your head slightly. Stay in this position for just 20 seconds. Engage your inner witness. Observe what this feels like.
- Now sit up and pay attention to your posture and see if there is a slouch, a curve, or tension somewhere. Do you hunch your shoulders? Check on the inner attitude that goes with it. Then straighten your spine, drop the tension, and see what happens as you do this. Do you feel a difference?
- Now *slowly* lift your posture as if you are being pulled up by the crown of your head. Drop your chin slightly and lengthen the back of your neck.
- Lift your chin ever so slightly. How is your mood? Any changes?

It's no secret that how we hold our body affects our mood and attitude. An awake posture allows for an awake mind! One study (Carney etal, 2010, Cuddy, 2013) even showed that when people posed in a powerful body position (e.g., standing tall and spreading their arms) for just 2 minutes, their testosterone (strength/dominance) levels went up and their cortisol (stress) hormones went down. In contrast the control group representing the less powerful body positions had an increase in Cortisol levels. Their stress levels went up.

Inner and Outer Posture

First and foremost, your body needs to be comfortable and alert. If your posture is restricted, your mind will also not be receptive toward your experience. But you don't want to be so comfortable that your body assumes sleepiness. I prefer the term *relaxed-alert*, a state in which your body is at ease—nothing is hurting or straining, and yet you are alert enough to pay attention.

There are two elements of posture: the structure of how you place your body in space, and your inner attitude of how you identify yourself (Johnson, 1996). For example, if you arrive at the exercise with anger and resentment, you will probably experience some tension in your body, such as a stiff neck or tense face. When you sit down to do your meditation, you will notice how your anger changes the shape of your body.

Reminder: Check Your Posture

When you do the exercises in this book, I will remind you to start by checking your posture, inner and outer. By making this slight adjustment to your posture, you will gain much more from the exercises, and you will spend less time in mental and physical states that don't serve you.

Getting Creative With Your Posture

Although each exercise in this book suggests a posture to match its requirements, please use your judgment to fit your body's needs. Some people assume that the sitting posture is the only one, but there are many we can use to practice. I like to mix up postures for several reasons. First, you want to be comfortable, so adjusting the posture to your particular needs is crucial. When you don't have to worry about your comfort, you will be more present for your practice. Second—and this may sound contradictory to the first point— if you are too comfortable, you will go to sleep. In other words, if you are always assuming the same routine and the same posture, you will get used to it, and the exercises will lose their effectiveness. Try an exercise, for example, lying down: You will have a different experience than you do when you perform the same exercise sitting up. This will engage your curiosity, and you will learn how to "be with" a tolerable amount of discomfort in a safe way. You might even find sitting challenging and feel as if you can't wait to lie down. I encourage you to lie down first and let the needs of your body relax, and then later sit up and notice what is so difficult for you.

Mindfulness is a great opportunity to learn how you are organized at every level. You can become aware of how you like to feel cozy by being surrounded with familiar routines. You can also discern how trying something new makes you unsure. This is one of the main practices of mindfulness: Can you tolerate various levels of discomfort and learn to accept them?

Mixing up the postures is also a great way to teach yourself not to get too complacent in your habits. I suggest you challenge yourself with some of the meditations in other postures and observe how they differ. It's important to help your body be as still and slow as possible (even when walking and moving) because your mind and attention need to settle in order to let go of any habitual patterns. Figuring this out may take some experimentation. A good mixture would be to do a period of sitting for 15 to 20 minutes, then get up and do walking meditation for 10 to 15 minutes, and then sit again for 10. You want to avoid getting stiff, holding on, or being preoccupied by discomfort.

Meditation while moving is a technique I use with clients and students who initially feel challenged by sitting. Walking meditation has been part of traditional meditation practice for thousands of years. But I encourage you to experiment with moving gently and slowly as an extension of walking meditation. Students often find it easier to start by standing and then notice a movement that wants to happen in the body and follow this slowly and mindfully. After a while, the mind can settle and it's easier to actually sit quietly. When there is a physical limitation such as back pain, it can also help to walk slowly. All the benefits of mindfulness will still be present. The goal here is to learn to become more mindful in your life so that you can access all the postures and movements of your body with comfort and awareness. You need to be flexible and work with your particular entry points, limitations, and needs. Listening carefully to what works is also a way to practice kindness toward yourself.

Choose an Approach: Sitting, Lying, Walking, Moving

Searching for the right posture is part of your mindfulness practice. You are learning what feels just right, and then when you have it just right, things change again. Change happens all the time, and how we relate to change is its own lesson on self-compassion and flexibility of mind. When I first started sitting to meditate, I found it challenging to sit very still. I was used to moving my body all the time with yoga, dancing, and sports. I would overcompensate and "hold still" instead of "stilling" my body. When you still the body, you make small adjustments. You notice how you are settling in, and you gently "wind down" until stillness becomes part of you. Think of a leaf falling from a tree: If you watch its spiraling movement to the ground, you will see it arrive at stillness. Imagine for a moment that you are like that leaf—falling, adjusting, and rustling until you land.

Sitting Upright: Three Options

1. Sit cross-legged on a firm cushion
2. Kneel on a meditation bench
3. Sit on a straight-backed chair

Sitting

The traditional meditation posture is the seated position. Make sure when you're sitting up that your spine is relaxed-alert. There should be no tension in the back, yet no slouching either. If, in the beginning, you need to lean against the back of a chair to get used to this posture, that's fine. Eventually try sitting with your back holding itself upright. Unless you have back pain, I encourage you to sit without the back support, as this will strengthen your muscles as well as your inner alignment. I often advise my students at the start to allow some very small movement adjustments so that the body doesn't become rigid. You are aiming for a regal posture that requires some effort to maintain, but not so much that you feel stiff.

Experiment with finding a comfortable seated position, as this will be your default position that your mind and body are most likely to benefit from. Find what works, but if you are dealing with body limitations or a tendency toward sleepiness, mix up the positions.

Once you get more serious and want to practice mindfulness regularly, I recommend getting a meditation cushion or a small, firm pillow that tilts your pelvis slightly forward. There are several kinds of cushions to choose from—some support the legs or have different heights. Place the pillow firmly underneath your seat, so you can rest comfortably and still for a short while. Avoid any pillow that you will sink into; you want a firm base that elevates you slightly.

If you sit on the floor with your pillow, make sure you have enough height so your legs won't fall asleep. Sit cross-legged in a relaxed manner. You can support your knees with a rolled-up towel so your hips can gently open and not strain. Adjust the height of the cushion until your knees are slightly lower than your hips.

If you can't sit cross-legged, it's fine to sit in a chair. Make sure the chair is firm as well. A soft sofa is not so good: You might have some back pain, and you'll also have a tendency to slouch. If you sit in a chair, make sure your feet touch the ground, or if you can't reach the ground with both feet, place a pillow underneath them. Your hips and legs will be more relaxed when they are supported. If you need back support, place a pillow at your back.

Find out what works for your body, but in general make sure your body is relaxed and supported; otherwise, you will be fighting strain during the exercises.

Finding "Relaxed-Alert"

The spine has a gentle curve, so the image of a perfectly straight spine is a misnomer. When we talk about a "straight spine," we mean an upright, relaxed-alert position. Imagine your spine as a string of pearls, gently curving inward in the lumbar area (lower back) and outward at the thoracic area (between the shoulders). Imagine this string of pearls being gently lifted through the top of your head. Your spine lengthens, your chest expands slightly, and your pelvis presses into the cushion. This "straight" spine is really a lengthened spine.

During the exercises, you will learn to correct your posture over and over by lengthening your spine. It's likely you will get involved in your thoughts and feelings and suddenly realize you're slouching and your chin is tucked in or your belly is compressed. When you notice this, very kindly remind yourself to straighten again. Also notice whether your mood lifts when you do so. Let your belly be at ease so your organs can rest more easily. We tend to hold a lot of tension in the belly, so make sure you're not sucking in your stomach. Think of how relaxed a baby's belly is: happy and round, with no tension.

Lying Down

Try lying flat on your back with pillows underneath your knees and head. Another good position is with your knees up and your feet on the floor. You can place a yoga strap around your knees so your feet won't slip and there is no tension in your legs. A position helpful for those who have back pain is with the legs slightly elevated on a chair or on pillows. Support your lower legs on the chair; that way your legs can rest and any tension in your lower back can ease. Make sure you support your head with a pillow.

You can also lie down sideways if you can't lie with a flat back. This also works well for pregnant women.

When you are lying down, the challenge is to be comfortable but not sleepy. If you become sleepy, change to a different posture: Sit up and notice how your sleepiness can be shifted. If you get tired and actually fall asleep, notice this and consider whether you might need a good sleep instead of a meditation. If this happens more often, you might want to avoid this posture.

Walking

As you walk, place your left hand loosely within your right hand and hold it around your belly/navel area. Your walk should be deliberate, with your eyes cast down just in front of you and not focused on anything or looking around. You want your walk to be very slow, and you want to be aware of each step. You are being with your internal experience even though you are moving through space. This is an excellent time to focus on breathing. Take one step at a time, literally. Make sure you walk in a quiet space with few or no distractions. As you walk, you might begin internally tracking by saying to yourself, *placing heel, placing ball of foot, lifting heel, lifting ball of foot, placing heel, placing ball of foot*, and so forth. This will help you to become more detailed in the actual placing of your feet. You might notice also whether you are placing the outside or inside of your foot first. Make sure you are not so slow so that the flow of your walk gets interrupted, yet not so fast that you can't notice how you're walking. Experiment and find a balance that works. Let your breath be natural. There is no need to coordinate the inhale and exhale with each step; experiment what works for you. Some people like to take an inhale and then step and exhale and do another step. See how you like to do your walking meditation. You do want a light awareness of your breathing, but mainly you want to be with the experience of walking.

Slow Movement

Assume a standing posture and let your arms and hands move very slowly. Focus on the movements with your breath and move so slowly that you can be truly present with each change. If you speed up the movement, it's possible you will not be fully present with your awareness. Don't forget to include your legs, feet, and the rest of your body when you're ready. It's easier to start with a stationary body and allow just your arms and hands and fingers to move, then progress to include the whole body. The challenge is to be fully aware of your body and breath and not get entertained or spaced out. The moving meditation is an extension of the sitting practice. You are moving stillness.

Move and Pause

One variation of the moving meditation is to move a little and then pause and notice, move a little again and pause again. In the pausing, you hold your body still in whatever shape you are in: like being a sculpture of whatever shape your body takes in that moment. You hold and notice. This can become a very intimate moment. As you feel your heartbeat and your breath, you can sense your body more closely.

Body Alignment

When sitting, walking, standing, or moving, keep your body in alignment and try to never strain your body. In the sitting position, being aligned means having the shoulders directly over the hips. When walking, you want to be upright and make sure that you're not hunching your shoulders or pushing your head forward. As described earlier, the alignment of your body often reveals your inner state, so catch and notice your alignment first before correcting it. If you're walking and notice that you're moving your feet in a heavy shuffle, you can ask yourself, *What kind of walk is this right now?* You might notice a thought and be entertained by it; meanwhile, you might be allowing your spine to slump, and perhaps your whole mood has changed. Realign your body and notice what that does. Do you feel more alert? Uplifted? Do you notice how you have been absent or how you have "checked out"? Let go and return to your correct alignment.

Meditation Positions Summary

SITTING
- Try a meditation cushion.

- When sitting in a chair, make sure the chair seat is firm and your feet touch the ground.
- Sit regally yet comfortably.
- Choose a sitting position you can maintain for a while.
- Align your shoulders over your hips.
- Keep your head level. Keep your chin slightly tucked, but at ease.
- Instead of "holding still," make small adjustments and allow your body to settle and come to stillness.
- Relax your belly.
- Turn your attention inward and to your breath.

FIND RELAXED-ALERT

- Imagine your spine as a string of pearls, softly curving in and out.
- Gently lift this string of pearls through the top of your head.
- When your spine lengthens, your chest expands, and your pelvis rotates slightly forward, this means your spine is lengthening or becoming "straight" (this is a small movement).
- Release any body tension. Allow your belly to be full and relaxed like a baby's belly.
- Turn your attention inside.

LYING DOWN

- Find the right lying-down position for you. There are many, including lying flat on your back with pillows underneath your knees and head; lying with your knees up and your feet on the floor; and lying sideways in a fetal position.
- Support your body position with pillows; support your head especially.
- Rest your body for comfort. If you are pregnant, you can rest sideways.

- Avoid falling asleep.
- Pay attention to your breath.

WALKING

- Walk slowly and deliberately, with your left hand held loosely within your right hand, and hold your hands at your belly/naval area in a relaxed manner.
- Your eyes should not focus on anything but be cast down just in front of you.
- Be aware of each step.
- Let your breath be natural; there is no need to coordinate it with the walking step.
- Focus or pay attention inside while walking.
- Include an awareness of your breath.

SLOW MOVEMENT

- Move the body in a deliberate way. Begin by letting your arms, fingers, and hands move very slowly.
- Include movement of the legs, feet, and rest of the body when you're ready.
- Experiment with standing, sitting, or lying down and moving.
- Focus on your breath while moving.

MOVE AND PAUSE

- Move a little, pause and notice; move again, pause, notice.
- When you pause, hold your body still like a sculpture.
- Wait for the next movement or impulse and experiment.

BODY ALIGNMENT

- Recheck your alignment periodically; this helps with sleepiness.
- Make sure that your body is aligned: In sitting, your shoul-

ders should be over your hips; in walking, you should be upright, not hunched, and your head shouldn't be pushed forward.

- Notice the lightness or heaviness of your step.
- Avoid any strain or tension.
- Change positions (e.g., from sitting to lying down) if the one you're attempting is too difficult to maintain.
- Stay tuned in to your body; check in with your alignment every so often.

Always the Breath: Begin and Return

Paying attention to your breath is essential when practicing mindfulness. It can help you gauge your current state of mind. As one teacher has observed, "When the breath wanders the mind is unsteady, but when the breath is still, so is the mind still." (Saraswati, 2000. You breathe differently according to what you're doing, thinking, and feeling. Healthy breathing is essential to a healthy mind. Your basic body chemistry is affected when you aren't breathing correctly; for example, by breathing in a dysregulated manner, you disturb the acid-base balance in your body (Litman, 2012). When you're anxious, you breathe fast and irregularly, which can lead to hypocapnia, or the loss of carbon dioxide. Long-term dysregulation of breathing can damage your health. You breathe freely when you're relaxed. The key is not to force the breath but to first notice how you're breathing and make adjustments that bring relaxation rather than effort.

You can learn how to read your own internal state by paying attention to the quality of your breath. A calm and centered breath is like a wave. A smooth, sequential breath has an up and down movement across the front of your body. Most people can feel their breath only in very localized areas, such as the upper chest. But when you are mindful and breathing without hindrance, your breath will feel effortless and smooth.

If you ever watch infants breathe, you can see that they have a wavelike breath. They haven't yet learned to stand, run, tighten against fear, or clench in anger. Their breathing is more like water rippling across the surface of a lake. This is what our natural and undisturbed breathing is like. When we breathe in this way, we feel happy and at peace. Regulated and calm breathing is about how we feel internally rather than how it looks externally. According to Litchfield (2007), "Good breathing is ultimately about 'embracing' instead of 'bracing.' " He describes how we can promote healthy breathing by focusing our awareness and breathing inside-in rather than outside-in.

A focused, mindful breath is different from your normal breathing. For example, if you recite an Ave Maria prayer or yoga mantra, it can brings down your respiration to six breaths per minute (Bernardi et al., 2001). This slow rate is needed to synchronize breathing and heart rhythm and improve your heart rate. Slowed breathing has a different effect than rapid breathing, as it restores a healing pattern in the body. In moments of slower breathing, you can enter a more heightened awareness of your body and mind.

During the exercises, you can experiment with breathing through your nose and through your mouth to determine which feels more comfortable. But I encourage you to breathe through your nose, as there are extra benefits, such as the ability to regulate the speed in which you inhale and exhale. This rhythm is important when you are stressed or anxious. It will help inflate your lungs and produce a calming effect on your nervous system. According to breathing specialists (Litman, 2012), breathing through your nose activates small movements in your neck joints. These joint movements create gentle movement throughout the whole scalp and nourish the central nervous system, relaxing the neck and shoulder region. After a few nose breaths, you may feel calmer. Breathing through the nose channels the air through all the sinuses and cools the pituitary gland, which helps regulate body temperature and condition the air before entering the lungs. Litman describes the resistance of breathing through the nose as healthy for the heart. The nose is the guardian of the lungs. The gentle pressure difference between your lungs and nose ensures that oxygen will reach your heart as well as provide more oxygen uptake to all the cells of the body. This gentle pressure and flow maintains the elasticity of the heart and lungs and improves overall heart health.

Another benefit of sustained breathing is the calmness that comes from engaging the parasympathetic nervous system. The parasympathetic branch controls the smooth muscles and blood vessels and the function of the body organs. When you breathe consciously, the parasympathetic nervous systems begins to promote a slower heartbeat, engaging the "digest and rest" phase of your body. This can be helpful at times when you become aware that your breathing is more agitated. By focusing on breathing, and especially breathing through your nose, you can take charge of your ability to calm and soothe yourself. You can try this anywhere: at a business call when you're feel agitated, while waiting at a stoplight in your car or on your bicycle, or at a lively sports competition. Try regulating your breathing by simply tuning in to it.

Tuning in to your breath also serves as a baseline indicator of what you need to do. First, you want to observe the breath that's already there without changing it. Simply allow your attention to be with the breath that is. If your breathing is shallow or fast-paced, see if you can first tune in to it and then slowly alter your breathing pace. I advise a gradual change rather than a big shift. For example, if your breathing is fast and shallow and happens in your chest, see if you can bring more breath volume into the neighboring areas of the chest instead of breathing into the belly right away. Try expanding the inhalation closer to the chest by breathing into the ribs or underneath the armpits. As you exhale, focus the breath downward and imagine there is a weight attached to it. Gradually feel how your breathing moves from shallow to deeper and more in the direction of the belly. Eventually you will be breathing into your belly. You are gently coaxing your body to slow and expand your breath.

Learn From Your Breathing

Often, if you simply stay with your breath, it will change and teach you what wants to happen. But sometimes it may be challenging to tune in to your breath, let alone accept where it is. To begin this process, I tell my clients and students, "Get into the neighborhood of your breath," meaning that you don't need to focus away from where the breath currently is, but find a small area such as underneath the armpits to focus it. Your body wants to breathe in a regular and smooth way. If the breath is held, shallow, fast, or in any way not flowing, you want to work with it. Maybe the shallow breathing reveals a feeling that has been pushed away? Maybe the fast-paced breathing is alerting you to a simmering anxiety? Accept what is happening first. Then, gently and kindly ask your body for a change.

Another helpful technique is to talk to the breath. Say to yourself, *I breathe in, I breathe out.* As you calmly and rhythmically repeat this, your breath and body will respond. This is a technique I taught my own children many years ago when they would get agitated. I would have them say aloud, "I breathe in, I breathe out. I breathe in, I get calm, I breathe out, I get peaceful." This works especially well with young children.

If you're still having difficulty following your breath, try the following technique: Count slowly to five as you breathe out. This will help you to slow your breathing and focus your mind. When you inhale, let it happen naturally without counting, and then repeat the counting as you exhale.

As we will understand and practice in later chapters of the book, our breathing helps regulate our emotional state. When you notice yourself getting agitated, try pausing to notice your breathing rhythm. What if you could take charge right now and "breathe into the neighborhood?" What if you could slowly calm your emotion through the breath and regulate it down to a relaxed state? Staying tuned to your breath can help you cut through the irritations of the day and become more even tempered.

More sophisticated breathing techniques can help you achieve an enhanced mental state by first seeing and feeling the breath in your chest, belly, and lower belly and then focusing the breath on specific regions of your body. Since your breath reaches every organ and every cell, how you breathe into these parts can influence health and wellness not only for the whole but also for the part. These breathing techniques can enhance awareness and wellness in the body as well as give your mind a break from busyness or constant input.

Exercise: Start With Simple Breath and Posture Awareness

 *10–15 minutes*

In the breathing section, please note that you will be pausing at the top of the exhale and the bottom of the inhale. These pauses are brief and are not about "holding" the breath, but simply resting your attention. This provides an opportunity for you to study the pause that come naturally in between breaths. Pay attention to what comes up for you.

1. Set the Right Frame
- Sit comfortably, either on a chair or cross-legged.
- Deliberately collapse your posture by letting your head fall toward your knees, then slowly straighten again.
- Find a position that feels "just right." Your chin will be tucked ever so slightly; your spine will be relaxed and straight. Once you find your posture, stop checking it.
- Note your inner posture and what attitude or intention you are bringing to this exercise.
- Take a moment to find your baseline. As you settle in, pay attention to what is present in your body, mind, and emotions. This will give you a reference point for what you may notice has changed later.

2. Stay and Study
- Now turn your attention to your breath. How are you breathing? What is the quality of the breath? Held? Short? Long? Smooth?
- Keep your awareness on your breath and slowly begin to count from one to five in your mind as you exhale. When you have fully exhaled, pause briefly in that moment of no breath.

- With the next inhale, count one to five and pause again at the top of the inhale. Let the pause be brief and easy. This is about studying the moment when there is a brief silence in your body and breath. Be curious about what happens in this moment.
- If it happens that as you slow your breath, the counts are longer than five, that's fine too. Trust your experience.
- If you're having difficulty keeping up with the counting, see if you can do it for three cycles and then let go of it. You may simply want to follow the natural rhythm of your breath. Continue this for a short while.

3. Anchor and Harvest
- Now let go of the counting and pay attention to what's happening in your body.
- Maintain a slight awareness of your posture. Stay here for a few minutes.
- What has changed in your breath awareness? Is the breath smoother? Any change in your mental state? Pay attention to subtle changes in your body, such as an absence of racing thoughts or a sense of well-being.
- If you find yourself feeling the same as when you started, you can repeat the breathing from the beginning of the exercise.
- Pay extra attention to how you exhale and inhale. Often people are not aware of how they may have been holding their breath or otherwise impeding their breathing.
- Be aware that, just as you can watch a movie while folding the laundry, eating, or knitting, you can be "doing" the breathing without being truly present with it.

Summary: Breathing Guidelines

- Pay attention to the breath as it is in this moment; take that baseline.
- Be curious about its quality, texture, and rhythm.

- Keep your attention on the breath; wait and observe.
- Get into the "neighborhood" of your breath; for example, feel the breath moving in your nose, throat, chest, or belly.
- If you get distracted, try these focusing tools: Count to five as you slowly exhale; inhale naturally or talk to the breath (*I breathe in, I breathe out*).
- Accept the distractions and thoughts and gently return to the breath.
- Find a natural way for the breath to flow. Avoid forcing anything.

If you notice that the breath is held or fast, try the following:

- Make one slight change, but be gentle and gradual, such as counting, pausing a little longer at the top and bottom of the breath.
- Let the breath be slower and more sustained by focusing on the exhale more than the inhale.
- Trust your breath! It can teach you how you're feeling in this moment.
- If it doesn't feel good or if you're getting tense, stop! The focus on your breathing should be helpful and not increase your tension.
- If there is any strain, let go and simply observe
- Be patient!

Reminder: If you remember your breath, you are connecting with your body. This is mindfulness right here and now. Again and again, you will forget and you will remember. Stay kind and gentle to yourself throughout this process. Your attention will wander away or you might forget. Just come back gently.

Mindfulness is a choice. When you choose to start with where you are, you have completed the most important step: getting started! From here, you can also choose to be wakeful, to be alert, and to participate in the world. Meditation is the training ground for sharpening mindfulness. It's a process, and it takes time to realize its benefits, but no matter if you are a veteran meditator or novice, you start where you are. This is the attitude we need to bring to our practice. This will open up curiosity about what we don't yet know. As Shunryu Suzuki, a well-known Zen teacher, famously said, "In the beginner's mind there are many possibilities, but in the expert's there are few."

Everyday Mindfulness Tip

Next time you find yourself irritated or uncomfortable, take a breath. Literally! Use the irritated or uncomfortable feeling as a reminder that you are actually meant to take a breath. It creates a little break and can become your personal pause button to reconsider your irritation or discomfort. Maybe you just received a challenging phone call or upsetting text message? Track your response. Is your body tense? Are you having an unpleasant internal dialogue? This would be a good time to pause, notice, return to your breath, and ease up. Irritation can be justified yet still be destructive because your heart rate naturally rises. Use this trigger to cue yourself to come back to your breath and body . It's the same with discomfort. Usually we want to make a change right away, or get away from it. Use this moment to pause, pay attention to your breath, and make one small change right now. Make the situation manageable. Does your mood improve? In short, use the irritation and discomfort as a personal messenger telling you that it's time to pause and breathe.

KEY 3

SLOW DOWN

If you want to go fast, slow down.   —Ron Kurtz

Discover the Natural State of Slow

Contemporary society operates at a breakneck pace. We devour the Internet at faster and faster speeds and demand that more and more information be at our fingertips at all times, day or night. We get impatient waiting in line or in traffic. The faster something is accomplished, the better. As a result, our attention spans have noticeably decreased in recent years. In a study (Rosen, 2012) the average American high school student, for example, sustaining attention in a classroom for 15 minutes would loose their focus after 3 minutes. At the 8–11 minute mark, the students had multiple computer windows open and their focus was the lowest. The discrepancy between the slower pace of aquiring learning and the fast pace of consuming media creates a loss of focus-sustainability. The value of slowing down is becoming forgotten, yet the yearning for peace and quiet is there in everyone I see in my professional and personal circles. Many express the need to learn how to become more mindful of their body and how to restore health and well-being. When we heal the body, we heal the mind and vice versa. Most clients I teach mindfulness to don't recognize that their mental states are imbalanced. They recognize stress, feel tension in the body, and notice how distracted they are or how they can't hold it together. They don't recognize that the way they think, the speed of their thoughts, or the quality of their attention adds to symptoms of physical stress.

Slowing down is the first and most essential ingredient of mindfulness. It's also often the hardest. We are immediately confronted with the obstacles and resistance of our own body and mind. We don't want to take the time, or we feel agitated, anxious, and bored when we do. It's true—feelings do become more vivid when we slow down, and often that is not a desired experience. The truth is, however, that our natural state of mind is peaceful and calm. When we find the rest that mindfulness can provide, our mind finds calmness without agitation. As a result, we experience less fear, worry, or anticipation. Our senses come alive, and we may find delight in how the natural world opens to us.

Desert Driving

On my very first trip to the desert, I had high hopes of discovering the magic of Joshua Tree National Park. As we approached the entrance to the park, the light started to fade and my friend accelerated, hurrying along the single-lane highway through the desert. Watching the passing landscape, I commented on how bleak it all looked. All I saw were a few shrubs, some bare rocks on dreary-looking sand, and not much life at all. I was disappointed. From the racing car, it looked as if the desert were a stark moonscape.

As we headed toward the campsite to set up for the night, my friend suddenly suggested that we stop and take a look. I didn't think this was a good idea. We needed to get to the campsite because the light was fading, the cool desert night was beginning to descend, and we had stuff to do. "Let's slow down and get out," he calmly replied. I decided to go along with him. The moment my feet touched the ground, I felt the softness of the earth beneath. Little puffs of fine sand rose with each step. The earth was buoyant in a way I had never felt before. I walked into the open space, and the "shrubs" revealed themselves. A spindly ocotillo plant offered intricate spiral designs adorned with small red, oval-shaped flowers. The patterns of the plants showcased both their hardiness and delicate beauty.

I was now able to appreciate what I couldn't see while speeding through the landscape. As I slowed, my breath calmed, my attention focused, and I was actually able to see, feel, and sense the surroundings. How kitschy, I thought to myself, as the opening scene from the movie *The Sound of Music* came rushing into my head: "The hills are alive . . ." But the funny thing was, it was true! As I slowed, I could actually take in what was there. Slowing down was my entrée into discovering what the desert was about: space!

Obstacles to Slowing Down

The first obstacles we may find in our path as we begin to slow down are mindtraps. These are all the ways we tell ourselves that our fast-paced life or business as usual is the better choice. Even though we might recognize it's not optimal, our habituation to the usual way of doing things is very strong. We want to stay with what is familiar and comfortable even if it's not healthy. Here are a variety of mindtraps you might recognize:

- *I don't need to slow down. I can manage.*
- *I don't have time.*
- *I won't get anything done when I slow down.*
- *I'm fine. I can think my way out of this situation.*
- *I just can't do it.*
- *This is boring, and it takes too long.*
- *I'm tired (or exhausted). How will I keep my eyes open?*
- *I won't be able to function.*
- *What I think is real. What I feel is not.*
- *I'll fall apart when I slow down because the feelings are overwhelming.*

If some of these statements are familiar, try to get curious about them. Often, when it comes to our own feelings, we are our own harshest critics, but this criticism can get in the way. In mindfulness practice, you will undoubtedly come up against your own judgments and beliefs. I suggest that you become curious about them, for there is no way around them. Judgments and criticism are based on beliefs, and beliefs are important; they show you how you have organized your inner world, based on past experiences. Some of these beliefs can be helpful; some can be limiting. Pay attention and examine them with kindness.

Try this:

One way to work with beliefs is write them down. Then ask yourself: *How have these beliefs impacted me? Have they been helpful? Are they still useful? How? Are any of the obstacles listed above familiar to me as beliefs I have about myself? How have they served me? How are they no longer useful?*

A goal of mindfulness can be to become more attuned, compassionate, and embodied. When we are calm and peaceful inside, we are more available to others and to ourselves. We become kinder and more aware. As we change on the inside, we begin to see what we need in order to change on the outside as well. Recognizing the mindtraps above or what has us stressed, sad, angry, and depressed is a vital aspect of practicing mindfulness. Please remember that these feelings, experiences, or beliefs are not the problem; they are exactly what we need to be working with. This is not therapy time, but simply training yourself to become aware of what is truthfully happening and to apply this truth to living a happier, more fulfilled life. It doesn't mean you will be always successful at it, but you are learning how to become more aware. Slowing down is the first step in this process because it lets you see, feel, and reflect. Without this awareness, you will simply live the same old patterns. As the saying goes, if you have a hammer, then every problem looks like a nail to you. If you don't take a look at the tools you've been using and try something new, you won't discover a better way of living.

You may confront a variety of obstacles while trying the exercises in this book. To set yourself up for success, please consider the following principles of mindfulness as tools to help you in this process.

Four Principles to Help You With Obstacles

1. *Reflecting on and recognizing imbalance is essential.* Take inventory of what feels out of balance in your life. What is not working? What is imbalanced? Do you feel there have been better times when you felt healthy and well? Are you far from those now? What would you like to restore to emotional health? Under Key 1, I invited you to take your baseline. This is another opportunity to do so.
2. *Mental health comes from the inside out and not the outside in.* Stress and mild to moderate anxiety and depression can be helped by mindfulness practice. Also, when you change how you feel inside, you directly impact your physical health.
3. *Curiosity is helpful and healthful.* Allow yourself to be open to whatever comes. It might be unexpected and unfamiliar. Noticing this means you are beginning to be mindful.
4. *Practice feeds positive change.* Make the time and space to practice the exercises. Commit to this. Even 5 minutes a day can make a difference.

Slow and Restore

You body was not built to be speedy all day long. Your autonomic nervous system is a symphony of continually shifting tempos and rhythms, with a sympathetic branch that enables you to quickly and actively respond and a parasympathetic branch that facilitates relaxation, integration, and restoration. You need the ebb and flow of both these systems so you can build resilience to the stressors in your life and not be worn down by speed or stuck in stasis. During my drive through the desert, I wasn't even aware how stressed I was and how activated my nerves were until I slowed down.

Your capacity to withstand stress works great, but only if you have a chance to be restored. Your stress only increases when you can't rest and heal. Slowing the body with certain, restorative yoga poses or slow movements has become more and more popular in Western culture. This is a great way to enter a mindful state. According to new evidence from researchers at Boston University Medical School (Streeter, Gerbarg, Saper, Ciraulo, & Brown, 2012), the effects of yogic breathing are profound. The muscular relaxation that comes from rhythmic breathing affects the brain and body. Blood supply to the muscles increases, the blood sugar level decreases, and metabolism becomes better regulated. There are also claims that focused breathing enhances the neuroplasticity of the brain (Balaji, Varne, & Ali, 2012).

When your body experiences focused and deliberate breathing, its ability to respond to stress improves dramatically within your autonomic nervous system, which regulates internal physiological states. Dr. Stephen Porges made a breakthrough discovery by understanding how we biologically process fight and flight responses, and more specifically, how the vagus nerve plays a central role in understanding this instinctual phenomena (Porges 2011). The branchlike vagal nerve runs from the brain stem and cerebellum in the skull into the viscera, heart, and abdominal organs. This "wandering nerve" (*vagus* means "wandering" in Latin) spreads 80 percent of its fibers across the tongue, pharynx, vocal cords, lungs, heart, stomach, intestines, and, most notably, the glands that produce antistress enzymes and hormones, which influence digestion and metabolism. The vagus nerve manages the body-mind connection and is the "highway" behind the "gut and heart" feelings in the body; it sends continous information from the body to the brain stem. The vagus nerve has two systems: first, the familiar fight-or-flight response, which engages the sympathetic nervous system and its adrenaline response, and second, the immobilization response, which results in shutting down, fainting, and dissociation. The primary purpose of these systems is to save your life in the face of a severe threat or trauma.

The vagus nerve sends sensory information from the body's organs upstream into the brain. The downward stream of information within the vagal nerve, from the brain to the body, communicates to the viscera whether it is safe and time to rest, or there is a dangerous situation. When you experience performance anxiety or fear, the vagus nerve is highly activated, sending impulses through the body. When you get that tingly feeling in your belly, this is your vagal nerve at work, sending strong signals of excitement, fight, or flight. Even if the performance anxiety is not actually a threat to your life, the vagus nerve might send that message. Upsetting emotions or a negative memory can activate the vagus nerve and the body response. The good news is that you can influence this upstream activation with breathing, yoga, and mindfulness awareness of your body. By slowly moving and breathing, the vagus nerve gets stimulated and sends regulating signals to the body and especially to the heart. This is called vagal tension (or tone) and refers to the biological activity of the vagus nerve. The result can be calming impulses and regulated emotions, reducing anxiety (Porges, 2011).

In a 2010 study, Kok and Frederickson discovered that loving-kindness promotes postive emotions and results in higher (i.e., healthier) vagal tension. This study indicated improved well-being and health through postive social connection. Dr. Porges discovered that our social engagement with one another is one of the ancient physiological circuits of making each other feel better through regulation. By making eye contact and engaging socially, we enhance positive connection and therefore influence vagal tension and reduce anxiety. Of course, this can go the other way if social connection enhances anxiety, especially if there have been negative associations in a relationhip. In general, however, without interpersonal trauma, being in close social connection with others improves our vagal tension and regulates emotional states. There are two kinds of vagal tension: high and low. People with high vagal tension are able to recover quickly from stress. They have the ability to move from stress to relaxation with no residue. People with low vagal tension do poorly under stress and have a low stress threshold. How the vagus nerve perfoms (as measured by heart rate variability) indicates stress levels in the body (Porges, 2011).

You can influence your vagal system with your breathing and mindful movement. When you inhale, your vagal tension slightly increases; when you exhale, it decreases. Therefore, when you exhale slowly, the vagus downregulates heart rate and blood pressure and brings a calmed state of mind.

Slow and Remember

Slowing down can also improve concentration and learning. I have seen the majority of my students improve in their studies when they spend time in body-mind exercises prior to learning. As they regulate their bodies into a state of relaxation and well-being, they discover that they can take charge of their own stress levels. Previously, they would rush into the classroom, their minds anticipating the next paper or test but not focusing effectively on the lesson or lecture. As the instructor, I had the liberty of starting my classes with 5 to 10 minutes of mindfulness or a body meditation, slowing them down. Of course, I was initially met with resistance: "This is a waste of time. Can't we just get to it? Why bother; let's move on." I would tell them this was an indication that their vagal nervous system was activated, but would gently persist and slow them down so they could feel, sense, laugh, or listen. I would then have a very present and relaxed audience. The students would be receptive, inquisitive, and engaged. Their vagal tensions were exercised to the degree that they could step out of their habituated stress and become more resilient, focused students. To this day I receive emails from former students who tell me my classses were one of very few where they not only had fun but could also remember the content. When we're relaxed and calm, we can remember.

Slowing down requires practice for it to become a new habit. It doesn't just come by itself. Remember, during my trip to the desert, if I hadn't slowed down, I would have missed the simple beauty all around me. Engaging the physiology of the body is the first step to calming the mind. This means literally stopping and listening to what is happening in your body right now. You can ask yourself what you are sensing and where this is in your body. The details of your physical experience in the present moment will reveal themselves to you.

Try this:

Imagine your vagus nerve: Think of it as an intricate network of tree branches extending from your inner ears throughout your entire body. This network connects with even smaller networks or branches that touch each of your organs. Imagine your breath sending gentle impulses through these branches. Envision that with conscious breathing, you are sending calming impulses through this network of tree branches. From head to toe, you are influencing your body.

What happens when you do this?

Five Ways to Slow Down

1. Engage the Body

Engaging with the body is what I tried to teach Rick, a young veteran, as a way to slow down and begin treating his symptoms of PTSD. He came to my office seeking relief from his depression and anxiety. He described a lifestyle that was flat and boring, and only on weekends would he have the "time of his life" with extensive drug use. He lived in these two extremes, distracting himself during the week with a dronelike existence and then literally speeding through the weekend from one thrill to another. We could say he was trying to feel his body, yet his means of doing so were extreme. My suggestion that he cultivate mindfulness was met with utter disbelief. It took eight months for Rick to experiment with slowing down and notice what was actually occurring.

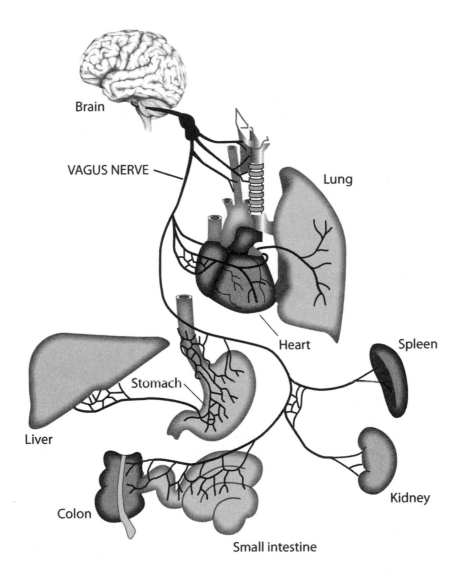

When he did, he experienced the sadness, grief, and trauma that had been lodged in his body-mind for years. As a young soldier, he had witnessed horrific events that caused trauma symptoms. To be calm, to sense, and to feel were frightening to him. He wanted to forget and live. He didn't want to slow down and sense his body because of the pain he wanted to escape. I suggested that he get curious and ask himself, *How am I experiencing myself?* and *Where is my body right now?*, and he found that these were questions he could stay with. He noticed the discrepancy between his weekday and weekend personalities and how, over time, this double life was not healthy for him. He also noticed that he wanted to feel his body but didn't know how. When he asked himself where his attention was located, he noticed it was always somewhere else— never here, never in the present moment. He described his experience as always wanting to leave. Once he could notice this, he became curious about why he felt that way. I then suggested he ask himself, *Why do I want to leave? Where am I going? If I do these dangerous activities, what will happen to me?* This young soldier got in touch with his fear of the memories and began to to slow down and be with his body awareness.

2. Recognize Fear

Calmness of mind is critical when we are faced with making life-changing decisions. Fear hijacks the thinking capacities of the brain and forces the body and mind into limited responses such as fight, flight, or freeze (Levine, 2010). With high levels of fear, the brain becomes overwhelmed and finds it challenging to contemplate any long-term decisions. When Rick's mind was in fear mode, he wasn't able to think through what he needed to do or how to prepare; he was just spinning in the fear, which resulted in an accelerated heart rate. His body took over; his mind felt out of control. His actions were then driven by this fear state, and he couldn't consider his mind or body. Rick was suffering from PTSD, but to a lesser degree we all can recognize the stifling effect of fear. When Rick began to recognize his fear, he also felt the sensations in his body. He noticed that his muscles were tight and that his jaw was clenched. When he slowed down to notice, he recognized the fear, and although it was not pleasant, he was able make the first move toward change.

Rick's next step was to focus his attention on his breath and slow it down. This made a direct impact on his physiological responses. This was not going back and processing the trauma; this was focusing on the present-moment body experience. When you consciously slow fast or accelerated breathing, you directly change the mental state that goes along with it. In one pivotal session, I asked Rick to place his awareness on his brain, heart, and belly so he could slow and synchronize his breath and awareness. Let's try this one now.

Exercise: Brain-Heart-Belly Sequence

 *15–25 minutes*

The brain, heart, and belly are three areas important for regulation of the body and feelings, since these organs hold the peptides and receptors that form the biological underpinnings of our emotional states. Engaged, focused breathing activates peptides and endorphins in the central nervous system and sends messages of well-being throughout the whole body (Pert, 2010). By conscious engagement of the breath in the regions of the brain, belly, and heart, the emotional body is calmed and restored.

1. Set the Right Frame
- You can perform this exercise lying down or sitting up. It may be helpful to do it lying down before bedtime to help you ease into rest. Or you can try it in an anxious moment, and it can remind you to return to yourself. Find relaxed-alert if you are sitting up, or a comfortable position if you are lying down.
- Allow your body to rest for a moment. What do you notice? What is your inner posture?
- With your hand, gently touch your forehead, your heart area,

and then your belly to cue your awareness. This means you are asking your body-mind to pay attention specifically to these areas.

2. Stay and Study
- Bring your attention to your forehead and send three or four gentle breaths toward that region of the body.
- Rest, allowing yourself to just notice.
- Touch your heart area. Let your breath expand into your chest area and into your heart for three or four breaths, slowly and calmly.
- Rest and pay attention to what comes up.Then rest your hands on your belly and breathe calmly into your belly for five breaths.
- You can repeat this sequence or just pause here and pay attention to what happens.

3. Anchor and Harvest
- After you finish the sequence, rest and notice whether you can feel a rhythm. It might be your breath, a heartbeat, or a sense of fluidity in your body.
- Hang out and appreciate what your rhythm is and how your body has slowed down.
- Anchor your experience by consciously naming what is different right now in your body.

3. Notice and Slow the Breath

Mindful awareness results in a more regulated breathing pattern with close attention to the rhythm of the breath. By bringing two kinds of attention together—the breath's rhythm and the mind's activity—the body can calm and body-mind awareness arises. Actively engage the breath in a more rhythmic, sustained, sloweddown manner, and the body will immediately respond.

This is your basic exercise. Notice and slow your breath down. It doesn't matter where you are. At any time, you can stop and tune in to what is happening. Noticing your breath is a good way to measure your current state. You can read yourself in this very moment and take a baseline: *Am I holding my breath? Where? Up in the chest? What goes with that? A feeling of anxiety? As I slow the breath down, does the anxiety ease?*

General Guidelines for Noticing and Breathing

- Notice what is, right now. Just stop and listen.
- Pay attention to where your breath goes. Neck? Throat? Chest? Belly? Brain?
- Name for yourself what the experience is (e.g., *I am stressed/anxious/content/down/sluggish*).
- Make an effort to slow this breath down. Focus on the exhalation and the rhythm of slowing.
- Track whether anything has changed.

Think of yourself as a scientist as you begin to work in this way with mindfulness. You are taking inventory of what is, trying something out, and then looking for the evidence of what has changed. If it's helpful, keep going. If it doesn't work for you, stop and inquire why. Most important, keep an open attitude and experiment. It can take some time to find your way to change.

When I introduced Rick to slowing down his breath, he experienced many challenges. First, he recognized that his body was impacted by fear and trauma. Painful memories that he was afraid of reliving would surface. However, by focusing on the present awareness of his breath, he was able to stabilize this anticipatory fear and separate it from the moment. He could see that it was part of a different experience. He began to feel a sense of control and ease. The dreaded fear of remembering was replaced by a sense of calm and well-being. By learning to slow down, he began to relinquish his need for excitement and constant stimulation and thereby to change his addictive behavior. He was replacing the habit of speed with the habit of slowing his physiology.

We don't need to suffer from trauma to benefit from working with our fear. If Rick can conquer his fear, so can you.

Exercise: Basic Slowing Down

 *15–20 minutes*

This exercise is a good practice to incorporate into your daily life as a way to slow down. If you can do this daily, you will develop healthy habits and train your brain to catch those speedy moments. The purpose of the exercise is to become present with the here and now and simply pay attention to whatever is happening.

1. Set the Right Frame

Posture
- Choose a comfortable place to sit. Make sure you will be undisturbed for the next 15 minutes.
- Sit upright, relaxed and alert. Find a balance in your body between sitting comfortably and having a slight effort in your spine to hold you upright. Imagine a tall tree or the presence of any person who makes you feel good.
- Or maybe just feel the lift through your torso and spine. You can also lean against the wall as a physical reminder that you are supported in the spine. Be aware of keeping a good posture. As you focus on your outer posture, see what your inner posture is like. Are they aligned? Different?

Eyes
- Either close your eyes or turn your gaze downward to minimize any visual stimuli.
- Keep your eyes soft and steady; let go of focusing on anything; don't strain your eyes.

Breath Awareness
- Is your breathing shallow, fast, or slow?
- Are you breathing mostly into your belly or into your chest?

2. Stay and Study

Focused Breath Attention
- Allow your breathing rhythm to slow. If needed, you can use the earlier counting techniques from the exercise under Key 2 ("Start With Simple Breath and Posture Awareness," p. 40).
- Gradually take deeper and slower breaths into your belly.
- Follow the air that enters your nostrils as it becomes a breath.
- Track how your exhaled breath turns into air as it leaves your nostrils.
- Focus your attention on the breath moving in and out.
- Trust the movement of your breath. It will slow you down.

Keeping Steady
- If your thoughts wander or if you get distracted, allow yourself to gently return to your breath.
- Keep returning, breathing slowly and deeply.
- Keep going for at least 5 to 7 minutes.

3. Anchor and Harvest

Linger and Notice
- Let go of the focused breath and just notice.
- Stay with a moment of quiet.
- Do you feel slowed down?

4. Listen to Your Internal Motivation

Why do you want to make a change? What doesn't work for you anymore? What do you want more of? After taking your baseline, you may already have an idea of how you want your life to be different, and maybe you have identified imbalances. What often stands in the way is failure to line up your motivation. To move forward, you need to recognize that some things in your life don't work for you. Decide what you want to change. You don't yet have to know how to get there. This is the beauty of working with mindfulness. You are learning a technology of inquiry that has been tested for over twenty-five hundred years. When the Buddha first sat down under a tree and discovered meditation, he was exhausted after a long quest to find out how to change suffering. He had tried everything, from one extreme of starving his body to another of indulging his senses. On his quest to find happiness, he discovered the middle way, a path that avoids both the extreme of asceticism and repression on the one hand and the extreme of indulgence and addiction on the other. He also tested it out for himself. He sat down under a tree and slowed down. He turned his attention inward, studied his experience, and discovered the wild display of his emotions, thoughts, and sensations. And he stayed inquisitive. He learned the hard way that if he jumped and turned with every new discovery, he would get lost, so he slowed even more. He stopped doing what he had done. From this still place, he could taste his experience without being dominated by it. In the same way, with practice, you can learn to touch your experience and then let it go.

What motivates you toward positive change? The motivation to slow down is highly personal. It might come in a moment when you catch yourself saying, *I don't want to keep going like this. I am not enjoying myself. Why am I stressing out like this? For what?* Another motivation could be, *I would like to be a more calm and patient parent* or *I want to savor my life, not just watch it speed by.*

On my own quest to learn how to slow down, I attended a retreat with a well-known monk. Five hundred people showed up. The main message for the week was for all of us stressed-out Westerners to relax and not take things so seriously. The week was filled with lovely motivational talks, nature walks, catered food, and lots of mindfulness meditation practice. Our meals were supposed to be a joy, the crowds a pleasure, and the teachings a blessing. As the week progressed, I felt more and more depressed, claustrophobic, and inept. I felt like a first-class failure at meditation. I imagined headlines about my becoming the first person to actually die while meditating. I realized my motivation: I was trying to model myself after a picture I had in my mind of a perfect meditation student. My fellow meditation students, the brilliant teacher, and my own idealized version of what slowing down meant all got in the way of my being present with myself. I had to find my own reason for being there.

What are your reasons for wanting to slow down? As you practice and listen inside, pay attention to the chatter in your mind—the obstacles. If they come up, gently say to yourself, *Thinking*. This will help you acknowledge the distractions. Every time they arrive, use this labeling technique. For now, simply practice slowing down, listening, and seeing what's there.

Exercise: Listen Inside

 *5–10 minutes*

This exercise is a quick one. You can do this "on the go" if you don't have much time. It incorporates elements of the earlier exercises. If you are unsure about how to tune in to your breath, you might want to go back to the section on simple breath awareness (p. 40).

1. Set the Right Frame
- Sit or lie down and get comfortable.
- Check your posture, and see if you are relaxed-alert. Make sure you body posture is aligned (if you are sitting up) or supported (if you are lying down).
- Tune in to your breath. Notice the quality of your breath, allowing it to just be.
- Close your eyes if you are comfortable doing so.

2. Stay and Study

- Internally say to yourself, *I am slowing down* or *It's okay to slow down.*
- Listen inside and repeat at least three times.
- There may be a negative or argumentative voice that finds all the reasons why that can't happen right now.
- Are these some of the mindtraps you have already identified? (p. 46). If you find yourself having an argument in your head, open your eyes and write it down.
- If you feel accepting of the slowing down voice, keep going and follow how your breath slows down.
- Then return to the exercise.
- Go back inside and repeat the statement, *I am slowing down.* Say it slowly. See what happens.

3. Anchor and Harvest

- Now let go of the voice and ask, *What tells me that I am slowed down?*
- Focus on your body. What is different? Are there any personal cues of slowness you can identify?

Note: If you still do not feel slowed down, repeat the exercise and pay extra attention to your breath. Remember that when you did the breath exercises, you practiced slowing your breathing by counting and focusing your attention on your breath. This will help. If you find yourself just too busy and distracted to slow down in this manner, that's okay. Part of mindfulness is accepting what is and becoming aware of what you're dealing with. There may be days you can easily enter into it and others where you can't. You are being mindful of how distracted you are. Have some kindness toward yourself in that moment. Remember, this is a process and it's valuable to understand what's going on. Try again later. This doesn't mean you "can't do it," but rather, *I didn't realize how much this arguing, thinking, busyness, and so forth is taking up mental space today.*

5. Mind or Body: Focus and Stay With It

When you begin to slow down, you may notice that you have a choice: to pay attention to what your mind is doing or attend to what your body is sensing and feeling. Ultimately, however, they work together as one unified awareness. When you sense your body, somatic messages come forth. For example, a tingling sensation down the spine might signal pleasure, a warmth in the belly may give you a feeling of satisfaction, or a tightness in the chest may signal an old sadness.

Experiences of the body are direct expressions of your moods and can be read like a language. Think of them as highways connecting you to the source of discomfort (e.g., muscle tension connects you to the emotional stress that caused it). In the same way, you can pay attention to pleasurable experiences. By noticing your body sensations, you can observe change happening. In mindfulness, keep your attention on the tension or pleasure. Focus and stay with it. Keep doing this simple instruction. This is one important path to getting through the habits and distractions. Come back and focus and stay.

What Gets In the Way

As you begin to practice mindfulness, a new set of obstacles may arise. Know that they are normal and happen to everyone who has ever sat down to reflect. It's what your mind does. Resistance is part of it. The trick is not to believe the resistance as the truth, but to be inquisitive and learn. Resistance can become a mindful teacher, pointing you toward areas in need of improvement.

Sample obstacles:

- *Carelessness or laziness:* Laziness is a very common obstacle. You may find yourself making excuses about why you can't practice today. Get savvy to your own laziness and see what obstructs your path to mindfulness.

- *Sleepiness/fatigue:* Sometimes you may just be tired and not realize it until you tune in to your body. If your body needs to rest, you might make that a priority. When you're sleepy, try raising your eye gaze. If you're drowsy, practice with your eyes open instead of closed.

- *Distraction/clinging:* This is a frazzled state. Here you might experience the tendency to jump around and not be able to focus. You might follow your thoughts and get lost. On the other hand, you might find yourself clinging to ideas, grudges, or stories.

- *Depression:* This state makes it hard to get motivated. There can be a feeling of dullness or of "nothing happening" in the meditations. Of course, if this persists, consult professional help (in Key 6, I talk more about when it's best to seek professional guidance).

- *Anxiety/stress:* You might feel tense or stressed out. Track the anxiety that gets in the way of feeling calm and inquisitive. Try practicing with your eyes closed instead of open.

- *Aversion/anger:* You might feel irritated. This emotionally charged state makes it difficult to be open to new learning. Irritation interrupts any attempts to settle and slow down.

- *Doubt/obsession:* These are repetitive thoughts that make it challenging to let go. You doubt your experience. Be patient with this state; it can point you toward what is deeply unsettling.

Try this:

Return to the mindtraps you identified earlier in the chapter. Are there any that you would add after trying more of the exercises? Are there obstacles listed above that you might add to your list of barriers? What motivates you to work through them?

When you slow down and start a mindfulness exercise, note what these obstacles are. Don't believe them; just take note. At this stage, noticing them is enough. Remember, obstacles are normal, and your job is to not give them too much energy. If you want to be more proactive about an obstacle, one strategy is to "check and drop." Say, for example, you notice an obstacle, such as the thought *I can't do this.* Make a mental check next to that statement and then drop it. You can visualize a wastebasket where you drop it in. Then you might notice the next thought: *What will this give me? It's no use.* Again make a mental check and drop it. See if this opens up more motivation to try to slow down rather than getting lost in excuses.

Slowing Down as a Way to Be

Brain research shows that mindfulness of your breath results in slowed brain wave activity and heart rate, which in turn brings a slowed inner state. The prefrontal cortex reengages in response to the sustained breath, and clear thinking returns. When you're engaged in mindfulness, this same area of the frontal brain creates little highways to the activated parts of your more primitive fight-or-flight circuitry, the amygdala. It's like building new neural highways, so new choice points emerge. The medial part of your prefrontal cortex has integrative functions, so when you understand and comprehend the emotional turmoil of your body and mind, you become calm and a sense of well-being returns (Siegel, 2010). Clients have described this sense of well-being in various ways, such as "calm," "fluid," "easy," "sweet," "coming home," "remembering a lost part of wellness," "returning," and "grounding."

When you practice slowing down, you begin to set the stage for your mindfulness practice to become part of your life. Learning how to slow down is the first step to discovering how you organize your emotions, sensations, and thought patterns. It's a valuable tool that enables you to inquire more deeply into who you are and can become the basis for lasting change. Remember my drive into the desert, and how I got in touch with the natural world and my natural mind? Feel yourself right now. Think of an authentic place that you are connected to and how you feel in your body when you remember. Spacious? At ease? The short practices in this chapter will help you to jumpstart your mindfulness awareness. Feel free to experiment and practice. Each time you repeat the exercises, you can discover new angles and insights.

Everyday Mindfulness Tip

Slow down in your body. At different times in your day, play with slowing down your activities. For example, walk a little slower to the bathroom and make it a walking meditation. Take an extra 5 minutes to walk mindfully to the café or sandwich shop during your lunch break. Sit down and have a meal instead of standing. *Take the time,* rather than buying into the idea that you don't have the time. Take the space. Linger for another moment at the checkout counter; take a look at the clerk's face and make contact. Resist the urge to go into action right away. Stop for a moment and notice your body. How are you experiencing your body right now? Listen to your breath. What comes into your attention when you slow down?

KEY 4

BEFRIEND YOUR BODY

The full benefits and fruition of meditation cannot be experienced or enjoyed when we are not grounded in our bodies.   —REGGIE RAY

With Keys 1 through 3, you are becoming familiar with mindfulness and discovering that you can slow down and notice your breath and body sensations. You may be saying, *What do I do now? What do I pay attention to? A lot is coming up for me. Do I entertain these ideas and make decisions about them, or do I just sit? It's so busy in there. I can't even be quiet for one minute.* Most meditators feel challenged at this stage because they don't know what to focus on. The idea of going inside and just noticing can be confusing, overwhelming, and even terrifying. In difficult moments like this, it can be helpful to actively engage your body. This will ground your meditation so that you can begin to understand the body as an experience of mindfulness in its own right. In fact, staying with the sensations of your body is the journey you are undertaking, one that will lead you to understand yourself apart from the seemingly incessant stream of beliefs, ideas, and judgments.

Because most of us are not fully attuned to the rhythms of healthy eating, sufficient sleep, and stress regulation, it's important for us to focus on the body. We often don't know when to turn down the relentless assault of electronic information and stimulation. But when we slow down and take the time to listen, our bodies can become a great resource. For instance, my client Cindy worked for years as a night nurse in a hospital. She had become so accustomed to this work rhythm that she didn't notice how it was affecting her health. She didn't realize that her symptoms of restlessness, insomnia, digestive disturbances, and tardiness for therapy appointments were related to a reversed circadian rhythm. She was used to the night routine she had created, but her body didn't agree with it. When she began to practice mindfulness, she began to tune in to her body and discover her fatigue and disconnect from the "normal flow of life," as she put it. Cindy began to listen to the sensations and feelings in her body, and they became a guide for her decision to change her work life.

Paying attention to stress symptoms in this way can help you attune to your body's interoception (internal state). During initial sessions, clients often describe how they brush aside stress symptoms, can't concentrate, or fail to pay attention to headaches, stomach aches, digestive problems, and the many other symptoms that tell them that their body is overwhelmed and needs a different pace. By learning to pay attention to physical cues as indicators of your health status, you can rely on your body as a compass that points to the healthiest direction.

In a study by Royal Holloway (Ainley, 2013), female volunteers ages nineteen to twenty-six took a perception test in which they had to count their own heartbeat, thus tuning in to their body's interoception. The objective of the study was to determine how women perceived their body image when they became aware of themselves from the outside versus the inside. In the study it was observed that when the women were more in touch with their bodies (and not perceiving themselves as objects), they were less likely to suffer from eating disorders and depression. Anecdotally, I have seen in my practice how learning to tune in to the cues of the body strengthens a sense of self-perception and well-being. Others may judge you, but this doesn't affect you as much when you're connected with how you feel on the inside.

You have also been learning with Keys 1, 2, and 3 that noticing without judgment is an essential part of practicing mindfulness. With Keys 4, 5, and 6, you will further develop the capacity to notice how you are and not judge or dwell on *why* you are, since the "why" may give you preconceived answers and get in the way of healthy change. Again and again, I encourage you to return to sensing your body and breath as a way to help you measure how you are doing in the present moment. This may be accompanied by some discomfort, but as you cultivate body and breath awareness, you may begin to tune in more often without judgment to the sensate and emotional terrain of your experience. With practice, you will be able to delve deeper into your physical and emotional states and discover mindful awareness during the most difficult moments. This should bring you more into balance as you gain the tools to be with yourself and make healthful choices.

Making Use of the Keys

To make the best use of Keys 4, 5, and 6, remember to slow down and track your experiences. If you are having difficulty with this, try revisiting earlier exercises. "Taking Your Baseline" (under Key 1) and "Basic Slowing Down" (under Key 3) can help ground you. Pace yourself and use the tools you have developed. Remember the guidelines of safety, listening, and practice (Key 1) as well as setting the right frame, "staying with it," and anchoring your experiences. These will help you as you dive in to what drives your daily fears, dreams, suffering, and curiosity.

Try this:

   At random times during the day—settling into your office chair, driving in your car, or walking to the store—check in with your body awareness. This takes just a few seconds. Say quietly to yourself, *How am I in my body right now?* If you notice impatience, hurry, irritation, or a feeling of not being in tune with your body, try the following: Take a breath and add a little kindness. This can be in the form of a gentle breath; sense how the breath flows in and out. Or it can be a kind statement to yourself as you breathe. Check in as many times during the day as you can remember. As you do so, note whether there is any change to your state of mind.

Meditating With the Body in Mind

Being in your body can be challenging, especially when you're hurting or in pain. However, even if you're not, you may be stressed, overwhelmed, or simply ignoring or denying what your body needs. As you focus on your body in your meditations, you may encounter the subtle ways in which you haven't been in touch. My students and clients have described this newfound awareness as "not being in my body." They notice that they aren't eating well or that they're neglecting their health. They avoid emotions or feel victimized by trauma or illness. They recount stories of abusing drugs or alcohol to numb the emotional pain of the past. Some describe not having any body awareness at all because they never learned how to be embodied or to appreciate the intelligence of their physical experiences. The bottom line is this: Most of us have a difficult time just being in our bodies (Ray, 2008b).

Although it can help to understand the *why* and *what* (i.e., the causes) of your unhealthy habits and addictions, the first priority is to use your inner witness and notice "how" you are when you're engaging in familiar patterns. This is called mindful attunement to what is, not what was. Rather than focusing on the past and defining yourself by these stories, I tell my clients, "Your story is precious, but it's not all of who you are and it does not need to say who you are becoming." Many of my clients have a history of trauma and extreme stress. They feel shame or guilt for having gone through unimaginable pain, both physical and emotional. For instance, as I worked with a client who was a scientist and who suffered from severe panic attacks and anxiety, we discovered that he had never considered his body as a place of comfort but rather a place of pain. By mindfully noticing his body throughout the day, he came to befriend his feelings and sensations and not be afraid of them. He began this process by first paying more attention to activities he loved doing. An avid roller-skater, he would take his mind off his worries by going for long rides after work. He began by paying attention to the joy he felt being in sync with his stride. This translated over time to the skill of "just paying attention" to all body states. He learned to focus and stay in the present moment, and when he had panic attacks, he was able to not be "panicked by the panic attack," but trust that his body's anxiety would subside when he focused on the present moment. In the process of learning to tolerate his anxiety, he came to understand the value of it, just as he valued the pleasure of his skating. His body was giving him cues about what was more helpful than stressful. He began to listen to his body as a resource that he could read to find out if he needed more exercise, sleep, time alone, or connection with friends and family.

Pausing to notice how your body is feeling in a difficult moment and being open to its response is an essential and helpful practice. When my children have had a stressful day, I often ask them to close their eyes and breathe into their body and notice what kind of day they really had—not the one they think they had, but the one their body had. Try this for a moment: Close your eyes, breathe into your belly, slow down, and notice what kind of day your body is having.

After pausing to feel and sense how you are physically in the moment, the second priority is to stay with the sensations long enough to tune in to what is needed. The good news is there is nothing more direct than working with the body: Its sensory feedback is immediate. Even if you don't consider your body a "friendly zone" at this time, it can still be helpful to sit with it. Or you might discover that tuning into your body is a comfortable and easy activity and that you can further build on this resource. You may do this more easily if you consider all sensations equal, whether they are hot, cold, tingling, sharp, sweet, or anything else. It is only in our minds that we create categories and labels such as good or bad, and these sensations are actually just information used by the body to tell you what you're feeling. For example, a tight shoulder may remind you of the stress that has been building for weeks. This simple awareness can help you breathe into the shoulder, to melt and soften, thereby helping to ease your tension just a little. This mindful attention may also offer a remedy. For example, this same tight shoulder may indicate that you are not feeling confident at your new job. Maybe the new situation is creating some mild stress that you are not aware of. By catching this physical cue, you can begin to address the issue. Perhaps you need to rally some support for your concerns. The body knows this, but you have to give it a chance to respond. Or you might find a warm, settled feeling in your body as you tune in to your belly and associate this with contentment. Can you dwell here and take it in further? Tuning in to the body can be both pleasant and unpleasant. The question is, can we be with it, not judge it, and take in what this moment has to offer?

I have also noticed that when clients are able to focus on their body in the moment, they often remark, "What was all the fuss about? Why did I get so stressed in the first place? This wasn't as difficult as I imagined!" Once you learn to pause, notice, and stay with bodily sensations, you will get used to your body giving you its message. With mindful attention, even a strange medical symptom can turn into a clue. For example, when Jeffrey, a retired lawyer, experienced new and unfamiliar symptoms his doctors couldn't explain, he dug deeper. He found that his headaches and restlessness revealed his apprehension about no longer having his career as the center of his life. He had been looking forward to spending his well-earned retirement on the golf course, traveling, and finally having time for a new relationship. But as retirement neared, he became plagued by headaches, agitation, and restlessness. When he mindfully asked his body what these were about, he discovered that he hadn't acknowledged how much he had loved his work all these years. Simply understanding the connection between his body symptoms and the feelings behind it helped him let go. He began to be kinder to his body symptoms rather than being annoyed by them.

Throughout this process, it's important to cultivate a relationship with your body by being gentle and kind to yourself; otherwise, negative judgments may creep in and prevent you from even wanting to pause and track your sensations. Of course, first you have to use the inner witness and notice your attitudes. When I taught graduate students body awareness and mindfulness, they realized how harsh they were being on themselves. For instance, they noticed that they considered certain body parts "too big" or "too small," and they observed a whole host of other unflattering judgments. One student later recalled that simply anticipating tuning in to her body was terrifying because she believed that this would confirm that she really was a bad person. Then the opposite happened. She noticed how harsh she was on her body, but when she let herself realize this, she cried, yearning to be more kind toward it. She was able to befriend the harshness and allow something softer to arise. Such feelings as kindness and gentleness can easily get squashed as the negative, internalized voices dominate. Many of us get stuck on a merry-go-round of cultural, societal, and familial messages that dictate a limiting view of ourselves. We believe these negative messages to be true. Beliefs are the internalized views we live by, but we don't have to follow them, especially when they are negative. The key is to become aware and realize that we have these body images and beliefs.

Try this:
Identify some familiar beliefs you have about your body. Write them down or reflect on them. How have they affected you and your relationships? What kind of body image do you have? Be kind as you pause and reflect on your body and what you believe about yourself. Then take a moment and tune in to your body right now. Can you soften any harsh voices? Can you embrace any admiring ones?

The following exercise can help you learn to relate to your body directly by regulating your breathing and helping you settle into your physical sensations. Repeat this practice many times, and it will guide you toward getting more comfortable with and deepening into an understanding of your body from the inside out. Whenever feelings or sensations arise, simply notice them and come back.

Exercise: Three-Part Breathing[1]

 *15–20 minutes*

This is a lying-down practice. You can do this sitting up if you wish, but the idea is to release the body into the ground and let go of any tension. This exercise is particularly helpful before beginning longer meditations. It can help drop you into a sense of stillness of the body, especially when you (later) sit upright and then find yourself unable to "just sit." This is a direct way to meditate with the body in mind, as it's easier to focus on the breath when the body is physically relaxed.

1. Set the Right Frame
- Find a comfortable position flat on your back, perhaps with pillows underneath your knees and head. If you can't lie on your back, I suggest sitting up and slightly reclining. You want a sense of the whole back of your body being supported. It is not ideal to lie on your side, but you can certainly experiment here.
- If you choose to sit upright, find relaxed-alert by imagining the string of pearls that is your spine being gently lifted through the top of your head. Let the belly be at ease.
- You will place your hands in three places: lower belly, lower ribs, upper chest. The hands cue the part of the body that you will breathe into.
- As always, breathe through your nose (see p. 37) and remember from Key 2 to "get into the neighborhood of your breath," (p. 39) meaning that you don't need to focus away from where the breath currently is, but find a small area such as the armpits to focus on.

---

1. adapted from R. A. Ray, 2008a

2. Stay and Study

- Place your hands on your lower belly while allowing both arms to relax and rest on the floor. Make sure there is no tension in your arms or body.
- Inhale into the belly underneath your hands as if you are gently inflating a balloon. Gently let the exhale ride down the length of your legs.
- Repeat this breath. Slowly inhale. Follow the breath that fills your belly, and at the top of the inhalation, gently exhale. See how the breath wants to move through your belly and into the ground.
- Repeat at least five times.
- Now move the hands to the second position, your lower ribs or upper belly area.
- Again, do the same breathing pattern: Slowly inhale, and at the top, slowly exhale. See if you can find your lateral breathing in this position—that is, where your ribs flare out on both sides. Let that happen. You will feel your belly expand. If this doesn't feel comfortable or if you have trouble with the expansion, take smaller and more manageable breaths.
- Take five more breaths in this position.
- Now move your hands to the top of your lungs and place your fingertips on your clavicle, or collarbone.
- Use the same breathing pattern and breathe into where your hands rest, into the upper chest and neck and toward your face. Pay attention to how your shoulder blades on the floor or at the back of your chair slide slightly downward. This prevents a tight feeling in the chest. This breath has an up-and-down quality. You may be able to feel all three areas—the lower belly, midchest, and upper chest—at this time. That is fine. Keep your focus on the upper chest.
- Take five more breaths in this position.
- Return to the first position with your hands on your lower belly. Breathe there for three or four more breaths.

3. Anchor and Harvest

- Now let go of the breath focus and let your breathing flow naturally. Become aware of what might feel different. Do you feel calmer? What is the overall sense in your body? Did this breathing help you in some way?
- Stay for a short while and be with your body awareness. Linger as long as you can to realize any results.

Breath as a Gateway

Recall a moment of happiness, such as a time when you received a gift or made someone smile with a small gesture of kindness. Maybe you cooked a special meal or enjoyed a friend's company. As you remember this time, does your breath become more relaxed or easy? Bringing awareness to your breath is an effective pathway into mindfulness, since the tension or well-being in your body is connected with how you are breathing. On the most basic level, just slowing down and noticing the quality of your breath can tell you about your emotional state. As you gently guide yourself there, you may want to ask, *How fast or slow am I breathing? Where is my breath right now? What parts of my body am I breathing into or not breathing into? What feelings are accompanying my breathing? Does paying attention to my breath help me get closer to what is actually happening?*

As you try this, avoid pursuing the big *why* question (e.g., *Why is my breath so fast? Why is this a problem? Why can I not feel anything in that part of my body?*). Understandably, you may gravitate toward wanting to know *why*, rather than exploring *how*, but asking why leads to more thinking and more explanations. Explaining an experience before you have fully allowed yourself to feel it can derail its possibilities. When you are being mindful, the *how* of the breath can become fresh and interesting—a piece of new information and a direct experience of your body unfiltered by ideas and theories. The *why* has its place later on as you learn to integrate your experiences by actively reflecting on them. You do want to make connections to your insights and new experiences afterward, but for now, allow the exercises to be what they are without having to categorize them. Then, later, see what meanings and thoughts arise.

A client once told a story that illustrates the use of mindful breathing in a potentially dangerous situation. Cindy was walking her dog on a sunny spring day when suddenly her attention was drawn to something in the bushes. Glancing over, she saw that her dog's snout was inches from a coiled rattlesnake. At that moment, she was aware of her breath and even noticed how calm she was as she assessed the situation. In order to grab her dog and get him to safety, she had to come close to the snake. Cindy was able to see the diamond pattern and the shine of its scales. The sound of its rattle was faint. She had heard stories about rattlesnakes, all negative, and she had good reason to be alarmed, but what struck her later was how calmly she was able to meet that moment. She was very aware of the acute situation but not panicked or alarmed. The heightened awareness of her breath made her very attuned to her body as well as the snake and her dog. Intuitively, Cindy's body knew that staying measured and even was a safe way to avoid being bitten.

Breath awareness helps you train your body to meet situations as they arise. The space that gets created in these moments opens up any clenched or resistant attitude of the mind so that you don't act on incorrect judgments or hastily formed opinions. Remember to return to your breath over and over again. This is the golden key to any mindfulness practice. And never be discouraged if you feel as if your breath is "not right." It takes some practice. Begin with just noticing and then stay with the feelings or sensations as you track them. You don't have to be afraid of intensity, and you don't have to triggered by dramatic or troubling experiences. It only takes a single, aware breath to return to the present moment.

Exercise: Soft Breath Awareness

 *15–20 minutes*

This meditation invites you to focus on your soft breath. Notice the subtleties of your inhalations and exhalations. The objective is to train yourself to come back to your breath and soften your body awareness. This is an essential skill when dealing with stress. Use it often.

1. Set the Right Frame

- Sit or lie down and get comfortable, just as you did in the last exercise. Check you inner and outer posture for alignment.
- Feel the solidity of the floor underneath your body or feet.
- If you are sitting, remember to keep your shoulders directly over your hips.

2. Stay and Study

- Breathe through your nose.
- Feel the quality of your breath. Is it fast, shallow, held, tight, flowing, at ease?
- Pay attention to its steady flow, in and out.
- Focus a little more on the longer exhalation.
- Allow your breathing to be as easy and unforced as you can by softening your focus on it. You are not forcing the breath but softening the feeling of it, moment by moment, taking out any strain. Perhaps think or say the word *soft* and imagine how a gentle, warm wind feels on your face.
- Be patient and give your body a chance to respond.
- Try bringing a soft focus once more.
- Allow a gradual change. This doesn't have to be a big shift.

3. Anchor and Harvest

- Let go and sense what has changed inside.
- How do you relate to your breath now?
- Has the quality changed at all?

- If you don't feel a change, stay connected with your experience as always and see what is present. Inquire gently, *What is interesting to me right now?*

Stay With the Sensation, Suspend the Story

Five-year-old Jake was playing with his friend Tate when they got into a squabble and Tate began pummeling Jake in the face and chest. When Tate finally stopped, Jake could still feel the blows. With his face red and slightly tingling, he started to cry. He felt frustrated and hurt. Tate's mother was annoyed. In a curt tone, she told Jake to stop crying, saying it was unnecessary, and Tate had already stopped bothering him. Jake abruptly stopped crying and widened his eyes, saying, "But that is what my body feels to do right now. It's healthy!" Who had the correct idea in this situation—the mother or the little boy? Many children are encouraged at an early age to shut down their expressions of emotion, but by letting it out, the five-year-old was actually claiming his body's natural response. The mother's shaming instruction was not unusual, but she was also transmitting the message that the body's responses are not valid and that a controlling mind rules. For her, the intensity or messiness of expressing feelings was not welcome.

Under Key 5, I will discuss in more detail the importance of emotions, but as you explore your body's sensations in this chapter, it is essential to recognize that the two are naturally paired. When something happens to you, you typically experience sensations first, and later you express the emotions, which give the experience its context or meaning. When Jake was hit by Tate, first he felt the blow to his chest, and then he cried as an expression of his hurt and frustration. Let's take another example: the physical sensation of a hot flush through the face. Soon after you sense this, we might think, *Why am I doing this?* or *I hope no one can see me.* You might scan for something familiar or safe or try to hide, or you might want to know what the flush means. Are you embarrassed, ashamed, angry, shy? There may be a frantic quality to your needing to "know," and you may end up reacting. In many cases, as seen with Tate's mother, there's the impulse to shut down the sensations. Why? Does either response help? I am suggesting a different route, that of first trusting sensations as they are. Just as Jake did, try having them, feeling them, sensing them. They won't last. Only afterward ponder their meaning.

Emotions and bodily sensations are inextricably intertwined and inform each other. Author Jill Bolte Taylor has described in a scientific way the relationship between emotions and sensations, explaining how emotions are biological stimulations that alert the brain and body to spring into action and serve the specific biological purpose of helping us to survive. An action may be prolonged in response, but the actual, initial feeling is quite fleeting. Anger, for example, pulses through the circuitry of the brain in 90 seconds. After this minute and a half, we begin to create a story around our anger and embellish it (Taylor, 2008), and if we react to this embellishment, the effects of our anger may last for days, months, or even years. What I hear most in my office from clients are stories of how a sense of injustice and shame continues even when the flash of anger is long gone. The suffering comes from remembering and retelling the story, thus triggering the brain and body into anger states. Of course, there may not be an immediate threat, physical sensation, or anything actually happening in the moment.

As humans, we are so used to naming and labeling everything that it can be difficult to suspend this tendency and relax into what's unknown or what we can't describe. We feel and sense the heat of anger in our face. Our neck shows red blotches from embarrassment or our mouth dries up in a moment of fear. Typically, we want to know what this intensity means right away. And, when we can't make immediate sense of it, we may feel lost, chaotic, disoriented. Most of us have no education or map for "just sensing" the sensations, which, as Dr. Bolte Taylor describes, are simply immediate and direct responses to our environment. Consider this: Emotions are smart, relevant, and always accurate if we don't start spinning a story around them. They are simply information, but their meaning is derived from what we make of them. Equally, our sensations are instant messengers of what is occurring right now. Learning to mindfully be with them can relieve us from habitual or destructive reactions.

I am suggesting two things here: First, we can tolerate the initial sensation and suspend our need to identify the emotion. When we can just "be" with the flush as a sensation and not as something we need to label, it will go away fairly quickly because our attention rests on it. Second, we will learn the sensation's true meaning when we are not biased toward quick conclusions, which are based on managing the experience, getting over it, or making assumptions based on data from the past.

Mindfulness trains you to get more comfortable suspending the story, being with the unknown, and examining more directly what is. Physical sensations (including your breath) are the magic gateway for that. Without context and story, the sensation of heat in your face is just the sensation of heat in your face. Any embarrassing story you could concoct in the moment is most likely a reference to the past and something that is long gone. Let's take Cindy's rattlesnake encounter, for instance: She had negative associations with rattlesnakes and usually felt afraid of them. But her body awareness in that moment told her differently. She instinctively knew that if she proceeded slowly and didn't make a sudden move, she would likely be okay. The encounter with the snake is a symbol for the things you encounter every day that can make you afraid: a new relationship, a new job, a change you're not sure about. The things you're afraid of are like snakes, potentially dangerous, but they don't have to be if you stay present and tune in to your body awareness for information. The current moment is always a fresh start. A flushed face does not have to become an embarrassing return to the past, and an encounter with a snake does not have to result in a trip to the emergency room.

In the mindfulness tradition I was trained in, the feelings and sensations of the body are regarded as intelligent expressions of who we are. Experiencing physical sensations without immediately attaching a story to them can become a way to be with ourselves. We can intimately understand the imprints life has left on us and then act with authenticity, clarity, and poise. Clients have described this experience as "coming back home," or feeling "more in tune with my life." They describe having no fear, only open curiosity about what is. Let's find a gentle way to begin.

Exercise: Moving Body Scan

 *10–15 minutes*

The moving body scan will help you to learn to stay with your sensations. In this exercise, you will find a baseline by moving very slowly, using what are called micro-movements. These should be barely visible from the outside. The goal is to inspire sensations by moving the spine ever so slightly, beginning at the head and then traveling down the body. The overall quality of movement should be slow and gentle. Think of swaying seaweed in the ocean or gentle ripples on a pond. The idea is to bring very small movements to your body that feel safe and comfortable so that you can "touch" your body from the inside out. By doing so, you can contact your body with your moving attention and get to feel and sense it in a new way. Stay curious and open as much as you can. This is an exercise for mindfully coming into relationship with sensations generated by spinal movements. You can include micro-movements throughout the rest of the body, but I suggest starting with small, contained movements along the spine and then assessing your comfort level.

1. Set the Right Frame
- I recommend that you sit or stand (lying down will restrict your movement).
- As you proceed through the exercise, pay attention to what is happening in your body. For example, if you could assign a temperature inside, what would it be? Or what kind of textures do you sense while moving?

2. Stay and Study

- Imagine gently swaying trees, an undulating fish moving slowly through water, or mist rising from a still lake.
- Now bring a small movement to the back of your head. Let the first vertebra of your neck gently rock, swaying side to side; make the movements small and barely visible. Make sure these movements feel good to you. If they don't, please use your judgment and stop. See where you feel energized, alive, or stuck. Allow your breath to gently to travel to the areas you are working with. Continue down the neck vertebrae. The back of the neck is an easy place to feel a side-to-side movement. Then try small up-and-down movements. Allow yourself to relax completely. Track how your breath changes as you move this way.
- Move your awareness down to your shoulders and chest. Make small movements through your chest cavity. Follow your exhale, and notice how your shoulders drop.
- Notice any expansion or relaxation that may arise.
- Travel to the upper back of the spine. Feel into each vertebra or the general region of the upper chest as you bring small movements here. Each vertebra can be moved very slightly by creating a slight micro-movement in your back. See how that works for you. Drop any effort here, relax into your body, and work with what is there. You are looking for a sense of flowing motion. Experiment here and see what feels good in your body.
- Let the small movements move down your spine to the middle sections and then the lower spine. Pay attention to where the movements want to go. Keep imagining that fish swimming slowly or the swaying tree. Do you feel any specific temperature?
- Allow your breath to be slow as well. Again, make sure that you keep the movements small and pleasurable. The goal is to get in touch with your body awareness.
- As you move gently down the spine, you might sense the rest

of the body respond. If you feel comfortable, allow small movements in the arms, hands, legs, and feet. Or you can just stay with the very internal sense of moving the spine. If you are feeling self-conscious, you can slow down even more and make the movements smaller or take a pause and see what comes up. No one has to notice this!

- Breathe, relax, and let go of any effort. If you notice tension, see if you can let it go.

3. Anchor and Harvest

- Let the micro-movements come to stillness and track what is now happening inside your body. Are your sensations stronger or more in focus? Where and how do you experience the sensations?
- Be with your experience and don't judge. Sit and pay attention. What are you curious about right now?
- Listen with an open attitude to how you are in your body right now.

Learning Your Somatic Markers

There are 30 seconds left. You aim, taking the deciding shot for your basketball team. The ball spins through the air and tips into the basket. Elation courses through your body. The next time you watch your favorite team play, you feel pleasure, anticipation, and excitement, as if you were on the court dribbling and shooting. The elated sensations of your body register as activated states of your own nervous system. Coupled in this way, these sensory-based memories are ready to be called up for future competitions. You now have a somatic (bodily) reference for an experience you previously might not have had. The next time you play basketball or watch your team, chances are you will feel these body sensations even faster. These somatic markers (Damasio, 1994) are physiological record keepers that create meaning out of your experience. Each time you have a meaningful experience, your body has one too.

We live with a constant stream of sensorial and emotional cues, and we navigate our world based on these cues, constantly responding and reacting to our environment mostly without conscious thought. When a physical sensation or emotional experience, pleasant or painful, gets so deeply imprinted in us that it resonates long after the event has passed, the somatic memory gives a sensorial context to the experience and can exert a powerful influence on our lives. We may encounter somatic markers without even knowing it. Although we think, reason, and abstract our experience with the marvelous ability of our brain's neocortex, we are primarily feeling and sensing animals, unconsciously responding and reacting with our bodies.

Try this:

When you experience a particularly pleasant experience, such as a lovely encounter with a friend, a playful exchange with an animal, or a weekend stroll through the park, mark it in your body awareness by asking yourself to record this moment in your body. Pause and take in the scenery like a camera snapshot. Observe the details of the autumn leaves, the kind eyes looking at you, or the feeling of happiness you are having right now. Record the details of this moment with your senses. You can still go ahead and take that literal photo, but you are also recording a sensory photo with your body. Recall this moment later in your writing, or tell a friend. Make the sensory snapshot as detailed as possible.

The Body Remembers

Sally knew she disliked basements, but she didn't understand why they felt so creepy and made her shudder. Every time she smelled the pungent odor of a mildewy basement, she would be overcome with feelings of fear and dread. Yet she was not aware how every time she sensed this, her body was propelled back to a familiar heaviness. As a child, Sally had lived with her grandfather and survived the terror of finding him collapsed in the basement. She remembered nothing of the actual event, but had been told the story many times of how he'd fallen down the stairs and lay there unconscious. She called out to him, but was too small to get help and too frightened to know what was happening. Two days later, she was found nestled into her grandfather's barely breathing body at the bottom of the stairs. He lived another week until his body gave out from the injuries sustained from the fall.

The funeral was rushed, and not much was explained to four-year-old Sally, who was thrust upon relatives she hadn't met before. Her world was turned upside down, and this event marked her new life beyond the memory of the loving grandfather she had known. The somatic memory of being with her beloved grandfather in the moldy-smelling basement became embedded in her brain and body. Every time she smelled anything remotely like the basement, she was overcome by the feelings associated with it. These sensorial memories of her grandfather's passing were not connected to their actual meaning until she began to allow herself to feel fear and dread. As an adult, she had avoided these heavy feelings by staying busy. With this newly understood sensorial cue, she could stay with this feeling of dread and discover deeper feelings underneath. Sadness and grief poured out until she began to piece together that her avoidance was connected with her unresolved grief. Allowing the full expression of feelings and sensations enabled her healing to begin. She was able to integrate her body experiences with her emotions. She began her healing by listening to her somatic markers and allowing her body to "tell" her the way she had recorded this traumatic event. Sally's integration came over time. As she acquainted herself with her somatic markers and learned how to read these body cues, she began to feel a steady improvement in her well-being. The story became more a remembrance of the past as opposed to a feeling in the present. The emotions surrounding this event became less vivid. This is not uncommon, because when traumatic events are mentally processed and emotionally metabolized, the past stays as a memory of the past, rather than being an emotional or physical trigger in the present.

Listening to Our Body Stories

Somatic memories, or the associated emotions you hold as profound experiences in your body, can also be thought of as body (soma) stories. Each major event in your life is held as shapes and memories in our tissues. Think back to a teacher you might have had as a child, and consider your associations, positive or negative. Notice your body when you think of him or her: What's the feeling? Is there a body story connected to this time? Do you recall a sensory experience, such as the teacher's voice, attitude, or actions? What happens for you as you remember? Consciously or unconsciously, you carry many of these stories, whether or not they are positive and supportive of your current values and life.

These somatic memories can sneak up on you as something vague you can't quite place—perhaps more of a tone than a feeling you can name. Yet, you might have a strong reaction. Often a scent, a visual cue, or a sound—all parts of the older (reptilian or mammalian) parts of your brain—can get triggered into a somatic memory. The associated feelings are stirred by this somatic memory and produce a feeling, which causes you to react. You may suddenly not feel well or want to get away, or you might be intensely attracted to the source of the trigger. Think about the smell of apple pie: This could be a lovely reminder of how your grandma made it for you and how much comfort you had from eating it, and you might also remember the connection with your grandma at the same time. Of course, another person might have a different association and the smell may rouse something else. Somatic memories are highly personal and specific but are often not fully realized. You may not always recognize how they drive your decision-making.

Unfortunately, many of your body stories are probably related to painful experiences where you have not been seen, heard, or loved by others. At these times, your response was likely to hide, grieve, feel shame, or smother your feelings. Without your knowing it, these experiences may have been left unresolved, resulting in the stories you live by. Recall Brad from Key 2 and the depression that resulted from his feeling rejected and unloved. His body showed the caved-in posture of a person who is sad and shut down.

Under Key 3, you met Rick, the soldier with symptoms of PTSD and a speedy lifestyle. Rick had unknowingly created a belief around his behavior and experiences and felt he needed to live as if there were no tomorrow. He didn't value himself or his feelings and relentlessly abused his body and mind. It wasn't until both Brad and Rick began to work with mindfulness that they found out that their bodies had much to say in the form of tears, grief, tension, and sensations that felt as if they were almost too much to bear. In this way, their bodies were telling them a story that had gone unheard. Taking action for positive change is the challenge of healing, but first you have to give your body a chance to be heard and felt. Then you may receive similar messages about loving yourself, being kind and compassionate, and slowing down to enjoy what you have. In both Brad's and Rick's cases, when they began to listen to their body's experience and acknowledge its pain, they began to step out of old perceptions. Fears from the past no longer had the same grip.

This kind of healing happens gradually. You may notice that certain fears no longer have the same sharpness or the hold over you they once had. By mindfully facing his fears, Rick regained a sense of needed control, and by acknowledging his pain, Brad softened his self-judgment. New body experiences are not that difficult to learn how to read. You just need to take the time to slow, listen, and breathe, so you can hear what your body has to say. I tell my clients that it's like learning a new language, only in this case the language (of your body) is one you simply forgot. The truth is that this body story is being told all the time, but most of the time you probably recycle old data and get stuck with what hasn't worked because you think of pain or discomfort as an obstacle that shouldn't be there. Instead, try to accept pain and discomfort as it is—as sensation.

Try this:

Close your eyes and notice your breath. Slow down for a
moment. Notice how your body feels. Track your temperature,
your comfort level, how your skin feels, where your breath is flowing or held. Then ask your body how it's doing. Ask this with a
kind and curious voice. See what comes back. Listen to its
authentic response—not what your ego wants to hear. Sometimes
a sensation in the body may answer, or a thought will come up
that is fresh and unfamiliar. Perhaps an image will arise. Wait
and notice.

Resourcing the Body

As you become aware of your pain, you can cultivate self-regulation
as a resource. Self-regulation is the ability to calm yourself after
you have a difficult or overwhelming emotional moment (Perry,
2004). Babies, for instance, learn to be soothed by the loving touch
and care of a parent. Repeated over and over, this learned experience with a loving caregiver becomes internalized as a positive
body memory, and both babies and adults can learn to do it for
themselves. An unconscious somatic memory such as this translates into the ability to calm oneself when upset, stay hopeful when
things feel bleak, or breathe when stressed. Put another way, self-
regulation is the ability to soothe one's nervous system into a state
of equilibrium.

Mindfulness practice can help you self-regulate by creating a
positive and mindful somatic marker (like a muscle or an internal
reference point) that you call up when you need to calm or soothe
yourself. Returning to the meditation posture is such a marker. The
repetition of sitting in the assumed mindfulness posture, in which
you align your shoulders, pelvis, and head, creates an instant "memory" for the body. Your body and mind somatically remember the
previous times. You return to your attention and breath and therefore create a somatic marker in a positive and healing way. The new
somatic marker is the bodily memory of the sitting posture.

One of the reasons it is so important to develop a regular meditation practice is the repetition of the assumed posture. Every time you "sit," the body recalls the physical shape, and your mind and body align faster each time. The time it takes to settle in and quiet down is not as long. You might notice that the discursive thinking is not as intense when you practice regularly. In contrast, if you have been away from regular mindfulness practice and then return, you might notice how busy and wild your mind is. But then you will somatically remember the potential for your calm, soothing self. You can trust this mechanism, and the mindful awareness you create will build further internal resources. As a result, you may more easily conjure up an image of your favorite beach spot, a walk in the earthy forest that you remember taking as a child, the way your body feels when you sail, or the way you feel petting your beloved dog or cat. These are all sensory resources, reminding you of what is good, healthy, and strong in you and enhancing your brain plasticity. Each time you practice mindfulness, your brain receives novel impulses that enliven your neural connectivity.

When you need help, you may feel that you want a larger body to assist you. The meditation that follows will help you scan the internal climate of your body in relation to a larger resource: the Earth. You know how it feels underneath your feet. Reminding your body that you belong to this planet can be very comforting. You can sink into it as a place of warmth and holding, one that holds and nourishes. I suggest you work with the Earth as a resource to help you drop in more deeply and connect with the sensations in your body.

Exercise: Breathing With the Earth in Mind[2]

 *15–25 minutes*

This is a practice of connecting to and feeling cared for by the Earth. If images arise that stop you, try to release them. You are

---

2. adapted from R. A. Ray, 2008a

working on letting your awareness relax and drop toward the ground beneath you. Allow your breath to become a steady, smooth, in-and-out rhythm.

When you work with this next layer of your body, see if you can trust your sensations and stay out of the stories as much as possible. Remember to track your breath. As you proceed, sense your moods, sensations, feelings, and temperature. These can vary from moment to moment and from day to day—and that's the point. You are never the same as you were before. You are a living, dynamic organism who responds to your environments, inside and out. When you are in your body, you return to a more natural state of mind—one that is calm and clear and in which you can separate the chatter of your thoughts from truly meaningful experiences.

1. Set the Right Frame
- Lie down on your back. Get comfortable and scan your body.
- Work with the inhale and exhale of your breath. On the out-breath, release any body tension.
- Scan your body for a place of tension. Send your breath to that area; this will heighten your awareness. Then, with the exhale, see if you can release any tension.
- Repeat this by choosing another place of tension. Again, breathe into the tension, and then release with the exhale.
- Gradually work your way through all your places of tension, breathing into the area and letting go each time.
- Be gentle and take you time, sensing how your body relaxes into the Earth underneath your body.
- Let go as much as you can. Follow what feels comfortable to you.

2. Stay and Study
- Now imagine your body is gently sinking into a warm, receptive Earth.
- You are softly dropping down with each out-breath. As you do so, observe what this is like for you. What is this Earth under-

neath you? Focus on your experience, not the idea of the Earth.

- Pay attention to any positive images or feelings that arise. Let them be and come back to your own body. If you encounter negative images or thoughts, let them go as much as you can by relaxing. Remember to label your thoughts as they arise and then let them go.
- On the in-breath, again let yourself feel your body.
- On the out-breath, release any tension and settle into the Earth.
- Let yourself drop deeper, release any body tension.
- Imagine sinking into a loving, warm pillow. Each out-breath brings you into a place where you are being held.
- Let your awareness continue to drop even further, as if you are dropping several feet, then several miles. With each out-breath, you are letting go.
- Is there a subtle, blissful experience when you drop into the Earth? What does this feel like to you? Does your body feel open? Can you trust your experience? Can you let go even more and release even the smallest tensions of your body?
- Come back to the wave of your smooth, in-and-out breath and let yourself completely rest into the Earth that is holding you. Is there a subtle sense of the Earth being loving to you and you loving the Earth? Can you sense that?
- If you find yourself resisting or having a difficult time, accept that this is happening and just lie on top of the Earth. Sometimes it's not so easy to allow yourself to drop down into it. Allow that to be okay. Recall how you softened your breath during the "Three-Part Breathing" exercise earlier in this chapter (p. 74). Remember how you placed your hands on your lower belly, chest, and lungs. This may help you here.

3. Anchor and Harvest
- Now let go of the exercise and rest. Sense into your body. What do you notice?
- Sit up slowly and then feel your connection with the Earth in

a seated position. Does it feel different? What is your sense of connection right now? What do you feel connected to?

- How do you experience your state of mind right now? Write down some of your observations.

Lessons From the Body

If you grew up in Western culture, you were taught to trust a reasoning mind, facts, and scientific evidence, not to listen to your body. You probably had no lessons in school to teach you to slow down and trust your bodily sensations; instead, you were most likely taught to shut down, hold in your emotions, and not express what you feel. You may have had the experience of being in a doctor's office because you were manifesting stress through physical symptoms, but the doctor or practitioner probably didn't ask what was going on in your life. The diagnosis was delivered, but the reason why the stress was there in the first place was not addressed. Because you live in a culture that often does not value the sensitivity and wisdom of the body and emotions, becoming mindful is a radical act, one that requires you to stand up for your inner life.

The more you slow down and listen to your body, the more its messages will become direct and clear. Mindfulness cultivates the sensitive art of deep listening. You can remove the filters of fear, vigilance, and anticipation and come into direct relationship with what *is* right now. There is a sense of goodness and rightness in this kind of knowledge. But, as mentioned already, it takes some courage to live this way. It also takes some discernment to see clearly and not judge your experiences. Learning from your body comes in many guises, and you need to be open to them when they come.

Many years ago my friend Sabine was diagnosed with a thyroid condition, and she and her husband Paul met with a well-known specialist to discuss the diagnosis. Without much conversation or in-depth examination, the doctor told them she had to have surgery because, according to his assessment, she fit the profile of a European who had lived within the radius of the Chernobyl radiation accident in 1986. To the doctor, she was a number, a statistic, but not an individual. Absent-mindedly, he pointed to the middle of her neck and told her husband that the thyroid gland needed to go. He never talked to Sabine directly. She was thirty years old and still hoped for an intact endocrine system so that she'd have no complications with a possible future pregnancy.

That night, dismayed by the doctor's cool and dismissive treatment, Sabine went home, cried, and listened to what her body had to say. She got quiet and, without much thought—as she was an artist by trade—made a rough drawing of her neck and thyroid as she was experiencing them through her tears and confusion. In the middle of her neck, she drew a small red dot at the bottom of the thyroid. She then asked her body if her thyroid was in trouble. The silent message from her body was "No problem detected." The red dot was a tight little ball, not something to worry about but a hot little place that needed expression.

A few weeks later, Sabine visited a second specialist. This time, the doctor listened carefully to her story and her concerns (she didn't mention her drawing). He ordered alternative tests and found that there was a small spot on the isthmus at the bottom of her thyroid, right where she had colored a small, red dot on her drawing weeks earlier. In fact, the x-ray looked eerily close to what Sabine had scribbled on her pad. The doctor took a biopsy of her red spot. A week later at the follow-up visit, he bounced into the consultation office with a big smile and said, "Go live your life; everything is fine." If Sabine hadn't listened to her body, she probably would have found herself under the knife of the surgeon and compromised her perfectly good health.

Years later, after Sabine had three children, she again was plagued by her thyroid. The pregnancies had imbalanced her body and she developed a growth in her thyroid tissue. She remembered her listening technique and again asked her body for information, but this time the information was different. She got a strong sense that she needed to do something. Upon closer examination, her medical team discovered a benign growth, and she opted for surgery to remove her thyroid. Sabine struggled for two years after the surgery to regain optimum health. She went into early premenopause but was able to stabilize her symptoms. In reflection, Sabine realized that her decision to listen to her body years earlier and not do the recommended surgery was the right call. Had she not listened, she might not have had the chance to become a mother.

Trust your body. If you retain nothing else from this book, I hope you take away this single, short message: Trust the experience of your body. Not the idea of your body, not what you think about your body, but the experience you are having inside your body. The way you feel when you gaze at a meadow covered with bright spring flowers. The warm feeling you have when you look into the face of your beloved. The satisfied sensation of your body after physical exertion. The alert body that notices when a situation is just not right. Or, as in Sabine's case, the somatic knowledge discovered through intuitive exploration.

There is no substitute for learning the wisdom of your own body. When you learn to listen to your body, you learn to trust your experiences. As you practice the exercises in this book, you will experience calm moments, blissful and insightful moments, and moments when you feel uniquely you. These are to be trusted. The more you have these experiences, the more you will be in your natural self and not in a triggered, reactive state, and the more you will be able to notice when you are not in balance. You can use your body's messages, stories, or cues as a wake-up call to come back to yourself. Your body is trustworthy, and it wants to be balanced and healthy. Let any moments of doubt, distrust, pain, and confusion be just that: simply moments. They will come and they will go. Return to the present moment, listen to your body, notice the breath, and befriend the sensations.

Everyday Mindfulness Tip

What if the sensations of your body could become a direct communication to yourself? Play with the idea of trusting your body in a restaurant. You want to order a certain food or drink. You are drawn to that double chocolate brownie that your friend is having or the special cocktail on the menu. It looks good, and enticing. Now pause, slow down, and ask your body if this is what it really wants. See what the answer is. This is about paying attention to what feels truly right for you, not about generating a guilty conscience. You might feel that you actually want this treat and be able to savor it, or you might recognize that you are eating for social reasons and not giving your body what it wants.

KEY 5

TRUST YOUR SENSATIONS,
TAME YOUR EMOTIONS

Let everything happen to you: Beauty and terror. Just keep going. No feeling is final.

—RAINER MARIA RILKE

Just as you worked with Key 4 to notice and befriend your physical sensations, you will work with Key 5 to get curious and suspend judgment about your emotions. Once again, slowing down is essential, but now allow yourself the adventure of getting to know the feelings you may not have previously felt or observed. The mindfulness journey is full of surprises, and you will need to be flexible, open, and accepting about what you find. You can even be open to resistance and the emotions you don't like.

Bringing mindfulness into your life as a regular practice can help you change your mental health and well-being by showing you how you organize your thinking and what you truly believe. You discover what matters inside and what needs focus, and step by step, moment by moment, you work on this. Because of the brain's amazing plasticity (at any age) and its ability to shift and adapt with each new encounter, you can grow with each experience that you knowingly embrace. Of course, you want to mindfully strengthen the experiences that are beneficial and let go of the emotional dramas that damage.

Seeing clearly your natural self instead of your triggered self, as described in Key 4, is part of the mindfulness journey. This isn't always easy, as you may come up against emotions you would prefer to push away. Whether you are aware of them or not, you are driven by strong feelings, and most of your decisions are based on how you feel. The key is to see emotions not as problems but as discerning helpers on the path toward a more balanced life. Tuning in to your sensations and your body feelings can be helpful in this process.

Cool Head Remembers

My teenage son was close to tears. Panic filled his chest and voice. It was 10:30 p.m., and he had been cramming for a big test on the Roman Empire he was supposed to take the next morning. One moment he was snuggling deep into his comforter, the next he was bolting upright in fear, proclaiming to have forgotten the name of an important emperor. "I need to remember!" he shouted. His emotions were running high during this "invasion of the body snatchers," as I call these moments when emotions hijack reason and recall. Clearly, this was the wrong time to make any parental point about going to bed on time in order to be well rested for tomorrow's test. Anyone who has ever been around teenagers knows that when the "body snatchers" arrive, the rationally thinking prefrontal cortex of the brain leaves fast and dramatically. Parents are left with erratic emotional displays that seem out of proportion to the circumstances.

"OK, sit up," I told him. "We are going to breathe and get the cool head back."

"What is that going to do?" he questioned, half pouting and half mad, but then sat up.

"Cool head remembers, busy head forgets," I calmly replied. "Let's breathe. Feel your seat bones; notice what you feel in your body."

"Freaked!" He peered at me from under one eye. Ignoring the teen sarcasm, I kept on guiding.

"Keep sensing into your body right now. Notice how your breath is, notice how fast, where inside your body you can feel it." My voice slowed down, I was talking quietly, almost in a monotone. Like any mother trying to soothe an upset child, I knew to use a different tone to encourage him to regulate his intense feelings. "Allow your body to be. Let's wait for the body and mind to catch up. Give this some space. Inhale . . . exhale . . . inhale . . . exhale . . . feel your body . . . keep going." After 3 minutes of this regulating activity, he opened his eyes.

"Gaius Julius Octavian! You're right, cool head remembers." He smiled and soon fell asleep.

Remember when you learned in the first chapters to simply stop and notice? This is helpful when working with intense emotional states. The habitual responses in these moments are unconscious. You go on autopilot and power through, getting upset, aggressive, or highly reactive. Triggered emotions are similar to threat experiences. You react without responding from a clear, considered internal place. I call this being in a trance or triggered self, where you are not engaging your inner witness, or, as in the case of my son, you are being "body-snatched." Notice and stop: That is the basic teaching here. What else is there to do? Keep going and once again fail? Since pushing through doesn't work, you might consider trying a new approach: Befriend what is. And yes, befriend even the most "ugly" feeling.

On a brain activity level, befriending your feelings means that you are employing your higher cortical (brain) functions and regulating your triggered amygdala. The amygdala, the brain's seat of emotions, helps to process sensory information and tells the body how to respond to that information. This response is what we call "emotion," and it works in tandem with your neocortex to give your experience context. The sensory information can be a pleasurable touch you are receiving from your loved one, where the sensory impulses through the skin trigger a feeling of being cared for. The prefrontal cortex then gives meaning to this sensory-emotional experience by labeling it "pleasurable" or "loved by this person." If the touch were being given by a complete stranger, the meaning of this experience would be dramatically different. Then the reasoning part of your brain might assign the label "threat" or "ally" (depending on the situation) and release hormones that helped you to react, such as adrenaline, which gets your muscles moving so as to help you find safety or defense.

Fortunately, your brain also has the inborn capacity to regulate your fight-or-flight reflex. One functional MRI study demonstrated this when subjects were asked to view three images: a neutral one, a negative one, and a reinterpretation of a negative picture. Brain scans showed that the amygdala was activated by negative or threatening associations. The mindful subjects were able to use the cortical (reasoning) regions of their brain by consciously working to recognize their emotions. They were then able to down-regulate their activated levels to a calm state (Modinos, Ormel, & Aleman, 2010).

Humans initially learn the skill of self-regulation through the loving attention of a parent whose emotional stability and love teach on a physical level how to "be with" emotions and sensations. In this way, self-regulation becomes the way we cope with the fluctuations of our nervous system. Even if you had no such loving parent, you can still teach yourself to self-regulate by re-educating your brain through mindful attention. Whenever you pause your emotional reactivity and replace it with a calming breath and attention to the moment, you train your amygdala to respond, not react.

Self-regulation, as demonstrated by my son and the mindful subjects of Modinos et al.'s study, is critical for emotional health and balance. When you are aware of your emotions, you become less vulnerable to the volatility and feelings of being overwhelmed that upheaval can bring. The brain and body can handle the intensity by regulation through mindfulness. This lessens the impact of stress on the body, and you become less prone to both physical and mental imbalance. Your reasoning capacity returns, and you increase your emotional resilience. Even small chunks of time, such as 20 minutes of meditation, 15 minutes of playful connection with a friend, or a half-hour nature walk, can replenish your attention capacity. When you take mindful breaks, you train your body and mind to become resilient and able to deal with stressors, good or bad. Even with positive stresses (such as giving birth, having too much work, or organizing a big celebration), you need to learn to regulate your body-mind states for emotional balance.

Befriending your feelings as a way to self-regulate means you come closer to what is actually happening in the present moment. Reacting emotionally rarely means you are dwelling in the here and now; in most cases, you are responding from an earlier template of past experiences, often negative, that has colored this moment. In the case of my son, he had recently struggled to succeed on tests, and the memory of those failures contributed to his anxiety. Perhaps you yourself were influenced by a painful argument that happened years ago. When you "stop, notice, and befriend," you may observe that the person you are reacting to is just a human being, and she may look more vulnerable. Or perhaps she is angry, and you can see the fear behind her eyes. But you won't notice this unless you change your way of approaching the situation. By directing mindful attention to the emotional situation, you will develop a capacity for self-witnessing and find a new perspective. Just as my son got untangled from an activated emotional state that blocked his view, you can get out of the unproductive emotional state you've become wrapped up in. Try it right now by scanning your emotions.

Exercise: Scan for Emotions

 *10–20 minutes*

In this exercise, you will work toward discerning what is sensation and what is emotion. After you clarify what emotion you're feeling, it is usually easier to just be with it without any value judgment or story line. At times you might wonder what is a feeling and what is a sensation. When that happens, you can come back to just sensing the basic state of your body by focusing on the quality of your breath, your temperature, the location of any tension, and where there is a sense of ease. Then turn your attention back to the feelings that are present.

1. Set the Right Frame

- Start with your body and breath awareness and take a baseline of where you are now.
- See if you can settle your body toward quietness.
- Check your inner and outer posture.
- If you are having trouble settling, try focusing on your breath alone. Give yourself time. If you can't settle and find that you're too agitated to proceed, take a break and come back to the exercise at a later point. Being aware that you are agitated is useful information.

2. Stay and Study

- When you have a sense of your body, let go of the sensation focus for a moment.
- Scan for your emotions: Which ones are present? Are they strong or mild? Do the emotions have a story? Is there something familiar about this emotion? What would you label this emotion?
- If it's difficult for you to identify the emotions, or if it's not clear what is physical sensation and what is an emotion, return to sensing your breath and your body. Try to find a place of ease. Then turn back to the feelings of the present moment. If you are unable to do this, relax and try again. Accept what is. Emotions can be elusive or strong. Try to relax and be curious.
- Ask yourself, *What is in the foreground of my awareness? What is in the background?* In other words, what captures your attention right away, as the foreground of a picture might? And then, when you wait and see, are there more feelings in the background that you were not aware of right away?
- Keep placing your attention on the emotion that catches your interest in the foreground.
- Now include your breath awareness. See if you can let go of the emotion in the foreground by easing the breath with an

exhalation. You can also imagine the emotion passing by, like a cloud drifting lazily through the sky.

- If a story involving this emotion develops, see if you can drop it and come back to the present moment. Use a soft exhalation to help you with that.

- This may be the hard part. You might find yourself very much in the emotion, and that is okay. Keep working toward softening, breathing, letting go. Be patient.

- Place your attention on what has been in the background. Maybe a more subtle emotion? Or maybe a more authentic expression different from the foreground emotion?

- Notice whether you get pulled back into what initially caught your attention.

- Return again to your breath and let go of any sense of urgency, as well as any impulse to do something. Repeat as many times as you like. See if you can become aware of a shift, such as a lessening of the emotion, the story fading, a new emotion arising, a distraction away from your focus, or the background emotion becoming a little clearer.

- Stay attentive and relaxed. Stay with the emotions that are present. Get curious and just be aware without feeding any story line. The goal here is to scan the emotions and see them as they are, not analyze them.

3. Anchor and Harvest

- Let go of the emotion focus and return to an open attention of awareness.

- Just sit and be with what is present.

- Refrain from making up a new meaning, such as, *Oh, I am sad because* . . . When you hear this commentary, return to your breath and let go.

- I suggest further anchoring this exercise by writing down any insights, especially if you have gotten a clear sense of any foreground or background emotions. You might also inquire what has been in the background that you have not yet paid attention to.

Emotions We Hold Hostage

Paul wasn't used to showing his emotions or even knowing what he felt. His family was a hardworking, friendly bunch who gathered for pleasant barbecues and holiday celebrations, but feelings were never discussed. It was an unspoken rule in the house that showing emotions was a sign of weakness. Feelings were not to be aired publicly and not to be engaged. When Paul came to couples' counseling, he rolled his eyes every time his wife talked about "my feelings." He would smirk with the corners of his mouth, look downward, and avoid his wife's gaze. Internally, he belittled emotions, and he was amused that other people had these "fuzzy feelings."

At the same time, his nine-year-old son was exhibiting aggressive behavior at school, and this was one of the issues that had brought the couple into therapy. Paul's wife described how their son wanted to be close to his dad. She was upset that Paul couldn't see their son's longing for his attention. Paul scoffed at her remark, saying, "I just want him to be tough. He whines a lot." Whenever the focus moved to Paul's relationship with his son, I could see that his emotions were so bottled up that he couldn't muster much tenderness. Evidently, anger and acting out had become the boy's way to get attention from his father. Emotional outbursts full of aggression and hostility were an everyday, unpleasant event in the household. No one in this family knew how to be with his or her emotions in an authentic way. The mom tried to show her emotions but would get triggered herself by the intense exchanges between father and son. It was as if the whole family was held hostage by way they acted out their feelings. At the same time, each of them longed for closeness. The denial of emotions in this household had taken a toll on everyone.

I asked Paul to scan his emotions and notice what he was feeling. After some practice, he began to realize how embarrassed and ashamed he felt to express his feelings. He equated feelings, especially tender ones, with weakness and being "less than." He also associated showing feelings with the possibility of being bullied.

He remembered his brothers teasing him as a boy when he cried. As the youngest of four sons, he was mocked for being the baby in the family, and he wanted to protect his son by not showing him much emotion. That way, he thought, his son wouldn't have to feel vulnerable. His son's need to connect with him triggered this deep shame in Paul, and his automatic impulse was to clamp down on it.

In my office, after the emotion scan, Paul got quiet and held back his tears. He mentioned that he could feel his chest "filling up." I asked him to gently pay attention to his chest and the feelings that were there. Both his wife and I sat in silence, allowing Paul to just have this moment of emotion without having to clamp it down. Paul sighed. "What is your experience right now?" I inquired.

"I feel grief and I miss my boy." Paul expressed this with a sense of tenderness. "I guess that's what he wants, huh?" He looked at his wife, who offered, "He just wants to know that it's okay to feel."

Do you recognize parts of yourself in these stories? As Paul? His son? His wife? We all have areas where we don't allow our full expression of feelings to be seen—often because we haven't stopped to notice what we are really feeling, or we have difficult feelings that go unacknowledged or ignored. The messages around what is okay to feel or express are deeply ingrained, but it's okay to feel, and it's often okay to express your feelings. I sometimes tell my clients, "Your emotions might not be elegant or suave, but they are valid and intelligent." Noticing them is the first step. You need to acknowledge that you have them. It can be a courageous moment when you face your sadness, grief, or resentment. You can gain mastery and poise as you get more comfortable accepting the emotions you are having. The second step is to get curious and be with the emotions that are there. You can then inquire about the messages you have received from others around the expression of your feelings and reflect in a more neutral way on what made you angry, sad, or ashamed. You have more inner witness capacity when you can acknowledge what is, as you are not fighting the intensity of the emotions or holding them back. Many of my clients are surprised to find that it actually takes a lot of effort *not* to "have" a feeling. Most of us feel relief once we can acknowledge what is emotionally truthful, even if it stings.

Try this:

When you want to transform your emotions, you also need to hold an attitude of acceptance. Notice whatever feeling you are having right now. No matter what it is, notice any resistance toward being kind and accepting of it. Does that help to ease the resistance just a little?

Emotions We Hide Behind

Gail was slightly sarcastic every time she spoke with her friends, who had come to tolerate her biting humor. A sudden tone of anger would tinge her voice and quickly be followed by a funny remark. She was able to hide her contempt toward others with her edgy remarks, yet her sour expression betrayed what she really felt. She was socially anxious, even clumsy at times, but she covered up her anxiety and contempt for others with a sarcastic persona. She could not openly share her judgment, and it was equally hidden from herself. Gail was trapped in her own inner anger, which blazed through occasionally when she perceived that she was being taken advantage of. The effects of her emotional hiding out were profound: People tolerated her and thought she was funny, yet no one really got close to her. She missed being in an intimate relationship, as shown by the resentful remarks she made about other couples around her. During one of our early sessions, I pointed out that she sounded angry. Her eyes flashed, giving me a stern stare, and then she cast them down quickly to deflect her anger into another joke, which destroyed the close moment we could have had. She believed that her anger was not welcome, and she had learned to couch her feelings into socially acceptable bits of entertainment, which kept her trapped and lonely. Gail hid her vulnerability and need for connection with others behind an ironic facade.

Like Gail, most of us favor certain emotions over others, but lack the awareness that we even do this: Happiness is best, we think, and pleasure is great in regular doses, but not too much. Negative feelings are not wanted. And the more challenging emotions such as anger, shame, guilt, fear, resentment, disgust, and even joy are deeply intertwined with our views of our immediate family, the cultural context we grew up in, and the social networks we belong to. As a result, we have developed an internal map of acceptable and unacceptable emotions. Gail, for example, used sarcasm to hide her anger. She was afraid of direct confrontations and knew something was amiss but couldn't express it directly. She came to therapy feeling, like so many others, that something was wrong with the world, but not with her. She was deeply afraid of close relationships but didn't know how to look at her fear.

When you become aware of this internal imprint, it can guide you toward a state of more openness and consideration of others. For example, you may become more able to keep from indulging in angry outbursts, or you may learn to recognize the impact of your emotions. As a result, you may begin to share more positive emotions with others. Additionally, when you examine emotions in the context of your mindfulness explorations, you begin to understand how you have made sense of your past hurts by setting up emotional hierarchies. These hierarchies include valuing some emotions over others, repressing the ones that are unwanted, or being overwhelmed by feelings. In Gail's case, she became aware of the layers of shame and fear underneath how she conducted herself in relationships. Her anger was in the foreground while her shame and fear were in the background.

Additionally, Gail felt clumsy and "out of her league" while dating. She didn't know how to take in physical closeness and felt uncomfortable with the sexual feelings in her body. In her mindfulness exploration, she had the first safe opportunity to explore all these feelings. With guidance and practice, she was able to identify how she would get triggered and see how she privileged her expression of sarcasm over all the more vulnerable emotions. Becoming aware of this pattern, she was able to pause when sarcasm arose so she could check in with herself and notice that she was actually afraid. This gave her the choice to be in the moment and change her habitual response. Instead of making a sarcastic remark, she could acknowledge to herself that she was feeling afraid of being rejected or not accepted by the other person. Gail discovered that her sarcasm indicated a fear of feeling lonely and disconnected. This became a personal barometer for when vulnerability showed up. She didn't magically drop her remarks, but she began to notice and identify her emotions correctly. In this way, Gail began to understand her inner emotional landscape, and rather than being at the mercy of her emotions, she was able to make choices.

Over time, she reported that she was taking the risk more often of not making the biting comments that came so easily to her. Rather, she would pay attention to how the other person was responding to her. These moments were hard for her, as she felt "naked" without her armor of sarcasm. As a result, she had more direct interactions that were not controlled by her funny style. At times, she said, this worked well and she felt closer to others, and at other times she felt how awkward it was to be in real conversations or notice how others were using a similar deflection strategy. Gail would often comment to me that she was relearning how to be a real and genuine person.

Exercise: Accepting and Releasing Any Emotion

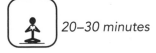 *20–30 minutes*

Suggestion: I suggest reading through this exercise first and then going through each step. As you work with your emotions, you might be tricked into wanting to find a solution right away; however, it's important to stay as nonjudgmental, spacious, and open as possible.

This is a basic formula for working toward acceptance and release of any emotion. Allow enough time in the setup phase of this exercise to ground your body. You might choose a more benign emotion or emotional memory to work with first as a way to get used to working directly with your emotions. Over time, you will feel more comfortable tackling more challenging ones. It's okay to start slow, beginning where you're at with no pressure; remove judgment and allow your curiosity to enter. Think of emotions as various and subtle hues of color that may take some time to see. For instance, it might not be so obvious at first that fear or sadness is present. This practice is about learning to lean into your emotions and accept them as they are. This may feel easy at times and impossible at others, for our emotions have been trained for many years and it's not easy to immediately unlearn our habits. Be patient and return to the exercise again and again. This is not about perfection but about being curious. Remember the jewel metaphor: You are discovering that your inner life, obstacles, emotions, and resistance are hidden gems.

As the poet Rilke said, "No feeling is final," but you can make your feelings last when you don't learn how to witness your expression of them. In fact, the intensity of emotions lessens when you can be with them. It may seem paradoxical or even self-indulgent to hang out with the feeling. But having the feeling, noticing it, and then actively witnessing it can transform it. In fact, it can't stay the same if you are aware of it. Most emotional difficulties stem from people not being fully aware, or not inquiring or pausing but being seduced into reacting. Another cause of emotional difficulties is the need to find relief from feelings. Consider that wanting immediate relief is a form of avoidance. It's natural to want to avoid, but that is only a temporary fix.

1. Set the Right Frame
- Sit upright and take a moment to settle your body. As you set the intention to work with your emotions, see if you feel calm, nervous, or open. Connect with your breath. What quality of

breath is here right now? How is your body feeling in this moment?

- Make this a safe exercise by grounding your body. Try to find a physical place in the body that feels good or safe. Breathe into this place and ground yourself, letting yourself become calm. Take time to establish this resource first.
- See if you can call up openness and curiosity in this moment by staying connected to your breath, your grounded physical body, and your attention in the present moment.

2. Stay and Study

- Articulate a feeling (it can be any feeling). Name it (internally or aloud). Perhaps recall an emotion you experienced in a recent conflict or situation. For now, start with a situation or memory that feels safe.
- Get curious about the actual feeling. Recall some of the details that surrounded the experience of the feeling, such as the environment, the person's face, your clothes, and the kind of day it was. Stay with the feeling that comes up rather than dissecting these details.
- You want to isolate the feeling's tone and texture, so stay with it as much as you can.
- Avoid looking for an answer or solution about why you are feeling this. Just allow it.
- Linger and hang out for a while. Get curious.
- Then directly ask the feeling, *Where do I sense you in my body? What are you trying to communicate to me?*
- You are not looking for an answer. This may be the tricky part, since it's easy to want to latch on to a solution. Instead, see if you can stay open to what comes up. There might be more feelings, an image, or a sensation.
- Stay open-minded and curious. What if this emotion you are exploring has something to communicate to you? Can you listen to yourself?
- Now let it go by breathing out gently. Say to yourself, *I see the*

anger [or other emotion], I feel it, I hang out with it, I accept it. If you are visual, you can imagine a soap bubble and the emotions inside it floating away from you.

- Keep imagining this letting go. You may also gently release the feeling by focusing on your breath. Exhale slowly, releasing any tension.
- If you are having trouble releasing, take a breath and say to yourself, *No emotion needs to get pushed away. Emotions are all valid. They change. They don't last.*
- The next step may be the most difficult part: Sit quietly and watch the emotion loosen its grip inside of you. You may have to repeat this step again and again. The habituation is strong, and you can easily get pulled right back in. If this happens, don't be discouraged; it may take more practice to allow the emotion to let go. Emotions are strong and you are invested in their truths, so be patient.
- Again, recognize that this feeling has a short life. No emotion lasts. They all move on.

3. Anchor and Harvest

- Let go of your focus and sit quietly for a few moments, noticing how you now feel.
- I recommend writing after this: Jot down what emotion came up and what you realized about it. Again, continue to be curious and not judge the emotion.

Try this:

When you find yourself triggered by an emotion, take a breath and remind yourself, "No emotion needs to get pushed away. Emotions are all valid. They change. They don't last." Then take a long, conscious exhale and come back to the present moment.

The Theatre of the Past: When the Drama Seems to Never End

Trevor had a shady past. After class one day, during a training I was leading, he came forward in tears. He had been touched by a lecture on practicing self-compassion and wanted to tell me his story. In the past, he had been a drug dealer and user, and in his youth he had committed robberies with his best friend to support his drug addictions. When his business dealings went dangerous and his best friend had an affair with his new wife, Trevor snapped. After almost killing his friend in a violent encounter, he realized he needed to get out of his hometown. His heart was broken. He left his friend, his wife, his family, his community. He developed a severe addiction and went broke trying to support his drug use. For fifteen years he meandered through the country, doing odd jobs and barely getting by. He eventually found a welcoming church community that provided food, shelter, and addiction counseling. He turned his life around and started to help others, counseling drug-addicted men who had experienced a similar fate. But the betrayal and hatred he felt for the friend who had "caused" all his suffering was still with him. Eventually, a message reached him that one of his family members had passed. As he returned to the hometown he had hastily left fifteen years before, he was gripped by conflicting feelings. Would he bump into his hated friend again? Was Trevor now better off than he was? Had his traitorous friend stayed with his ex? When he got to his hometown, he learned quickly that his friend had died the week he left—over fifteen years before!

"I lived with the ghost of anger for all those years," Trevor told me. "Every day I hated my best friend, and seethed in grief and anger, but for what? None of it was real." Trevor was overcome with longing and regret. Sitting quietly by his friend's grave that night, he asked for forgiveness, finally making peace with the ghost of his own anger.

The guilt of doing something wrong or the shame for being wrong can have a powerful impact on our psyche. We want to hide, avoid, get away, or go on the attack for feeling so badly. As I witness my clients grapple with emotions that seem to be as big as life or death, I kindly remind them, "It's just the theatre of the past."

Our emotions have a convincing yet ephemeral quality; the drama and high notes display themselves in full color, and the feelings make us believe that they will last forever. We suffer like the main characters of a dramatic story with unfulfilled longing and deep angst. Yet, in a flash, it's over and we are left with the imprint of the drama and perhaps a bittersweet taste. Even when we are mindful, the theatricality of our emotions is still there, but we can learn how to see through the intensity as a temporary and necessary part of befriending our feelings. We can learn to see, feel, and accept what is, and not be engulfed by the dramatic display. We can remind ourselves that this too won't last. When we let go of the struggle against the emotions we have deemed unacceptable, we open to the present moment and its feelings and sensations. We are taught by our own body awareness, a precious teacher, right inside us and always available.

Trevor learned the hard way. His journey through addiction and recovery taught him how he had neglected not only his health, but also, and more importantly, the wisdom of his body. He had not listened and had repressed his fears. It took Trevor years to finally come into a sustainable relationship with his body that was gentle and respectful to himself.

Try this:

Reflect for a moment on Trevor's story. What ghosts of the past are part of your story? Are there people or actions that you are not proud of that are still present for you today? Is there a gentle way you can allow these dramas of the past to be touched as you sit quietly? Can you acknowledge the feelings that accompany them?

Welcoming Difficult Emotions

Behind any good and juicy emotions are truths you may have a hard time looking at. When you engage with these emotions and learn how to read them, they can become a great asset in self-discovery and mental health. In a study of beginning and advanced meditators, participants ranging in age from twenty-four to sixty-four were asked to track their moods and self-awareness levels over a five-day period. After mindfulness practice, they showed a general increase in positive mood and self-awareness as well as decreased stress (Easterlin & Cardena, 1999).

Emotions want to be acknowledged. They have a right to be. Your emotional life is smart and often precisely attuned to what you encounter. Why not make your emotions your friends and learn from this intelligence? Remember from the last chapter that your physical sensations are trustworthy. You can equally trust any emotion if you learn how to carefully work with its expression. If you have a moment of mindfulness in the middle of strong emotions, you are learning not to react in ways that might be damaging to yourself or others. For instance, anger that is not regulated can be hurtful and turn into rage against another, but anger may also have an intelligent message for you—that is, if you can stop, notice, and not react. The intelligent use of any emotion entails actually feeling as well as creating a pause so you can become aware. With this pause, you can understand the meaning of the anger or other emotion and step out of the reactivity. Maybe the anger is an expression of outrage at an injustice or a keen observation of wrongdoing. But you can't find out what the true meaning is if you are seeking instant gratification for the anger by acting out. If you let go of the need to react or relieve the intensity, you can begin to understand the wisdom of your emotions.

Even children can learn to stop, notice, and not react to strong emotions. When I was invited to guest-teach a lesson on bullying and emotions in my son's third-grade class, I taught the kids a phrase they immediately grasped: "Cool it, chill it, breathe it— then speak it." These third-grade students learned that their feelings of anger and impulsivity were their responsibility and that they needed to give their anger a little break so it didn't become hurtful to others. They knew that the trouble with anger was how intense and hurtful it could be when it came out, especially when it took the form of blame. We discussed how other people can "make us feel this way." I told them that the notion that "other people are responsible for my feelings" is common and doesn't allow for the owner of the emotion to take responsibility. We often want to express feelings when they are positive and unload them if they are negative. We often "believe" our feelings and become reactive and then act out. The intensity of our emotions makes us believe it's right to do so. But what is happening is that we are being swept along in the emotion, as if it were rapids on a river. Because it's so strong and in the forefront of our awareness, we mistake this as a truthful moment. What we don't account for is that the amygdala is alarmed and simply doing its job by telling us how strong this experience is. The calmer parts of our brain, such as the prefrontal cortex, which help us put experience into perspective, are drowned out by such intensity. If we repeat this pattern over time, we start thinking this must be the right way to deal with our emotions.

What we need to do is notice that there is a high activation or intensity level in the body and know we can lessen it before we speak or make decisions. Since emotions can register on a body-mind level as mild threat experiences, we may react in survival mode, unaware that we have choices. When I asked the third graders to reflect on angry moments, they had a more balanced story to tell: "Well, I took his pen because I wanted it; it had my favorite superhero on it. But he grabbed it back and scratched my hand, and so I yelled at him." By analyzing this moment, it became apparent that there were several small survival moments for both children: One child was surprised when another snatched her possession, thus alerting her fighting response; thus, the child grabbed the pen back and scratched the other child. Being physically harmed in any way, such as by receiving a small scratch, also alerts a fighting or fleeing response (e.g., yelling). The internal experience is what matters. It is experienced as a threat, and the responses of the body follow quickly. One can only reflect wisely on the rightness or wrongness of a certain course of action (such as taking the pen back) when the body is calmed and the threat is over. My conclusion here is that we spend far more time internally and emotionally threatened than we are aware of. Instead, treat emotions as an asset to respond to, not react to, just as you would your ability to reason or take action.

Although children are still developing their brain's capacity to reason, they are capable of mindfulness, and mindfulness has proven effective in helping young children regulate their emotions. When they are gently coached to first name and then understand the impact of their feelings, they can ease the intensity of their emotions and learn how to diffuse the situation. In the heat of our emotions, many of us often don't consider the impact of our actions on others. Kids grasp this right away: Negative feelings don't feel good on the receiving end. We can learn the skill of containing feelings by not unloading feelings onto others but by "having" the feelings first. Become aware, breathe, and calm the intensity of your emotions before acting.

Try this:

In the middle of a conversation with a friend or family member, stop and take a break from your usual back-and -forth conversation. Switch into a mode of active listening rather than responding. Pay attention to your friend's emotions and body posture. For a moment, consider his or her facial expressions and feelings as intelligence. Does that change how you feel about him or her? What is it like to be receiving your friend mindfully?

Listening to the Wisdom of Emotions

Think of emotions as wise parts of yourself. You can learn to appreciate them and what they are actually telling you. It takes some reflection and mindfulness practice to unhook from needing to relieve the emotions, see what they stand for, and discern the best response. In this section, I explore a sampler menu of emotions. Since a detailed discussion of feelings and their manifestations in all their complexity as well as how to work with each one of them is beyond the scope of this book, it is my hope that you will sample a few here and understand that they are all workable. I will highlight a few here so you can engage with the basic notion that emotions are healthy expressions that you can turn into allies in your pursuit of well-being. You can then explore for yourself how to engage the intelligence of other emotions that may not be mentioned here. In the sections that follow, I describe the outstanding qualities of each of six emotions and offer a viewpoint for you to consider. There are also brief practices and hints to help you see the intelligence of each emotion. The emotions I picked here are the more challenging ones, since they give the most trouble. But as you consider this sample list, think also about equanimity, happiness, contentment, and generosity. They are equally important, and it can even be challenging to truly live in, for instance, happiness. Try on the idea that emotions are wise, and let's explore a few of them here.

Shame: Showing You What Is Wrong

Shame is the intense and painful feeling that you are flawed and therefore unworthy of acceptance and belonging (Brown, 2010). It's an involuntary response that just happens and takes over your body. Often when I look deeply with my clients at what's underneath emotions such as anger, hurt, or fear, we discover a deep shame about who they are. Guilt is a bit different. It's about what you have *done* wrong, whereas shame is the feeling that you *are* wrong and touches the deepest level of your being.

A client, Kathleen, recounted one such shameful moment in my office. "As I was setting up the table for the celebration, I snuck a cookie into my mouth. The woman setting up with me called me greedy. She said, 'Why do you always have to be so greedy?' Her face was angry and her eyebrows were all furrowed, you know."

Kathleen recounted this story with a shy smile on her face and mimicked the woman's expression.

"What did you say back to her?" I asked.

"Nothing. I said nothing," Kathleen responded, "I just walked away. But the cookie was dry in my mouth." She tilted her head to the side and cast her eyes down, as if to avoid my gaze. I noticed something carefully honed in that movement. Kathleen's mouth still had that social smile, yet her head and eyes told a different message. The story she had just told became uncomfortable between us, and her implicit message was that we shouldn't mention it further, that we should just move on and talk about something else. I noticed that everything inside me wanted to move on as if nothing had been said.

I had seen this expression before: a slight angle of the head with the eyes gazing away and downward, indicating a desire to change the topic. Kathleen was feeling ashamed for having been shamed. Her emotions were taken over by her body's need in the moment to protect itself, withdraw, and hide, as a survival strategy. As empathic beings, we humans mirror emotions. We feel what others feel. We also respond unconsciously to the inner workings of shame by agreeing not to notice. We turn away when someone else feels ashamed and pretend it didn't happen.

With Kathleen, I noticed that I felt the very same shame. The heat in my face was rising, as if I too had done something wrong. This is the powerful effect of shame: Inside, we cringe and beg, *Please let the earth open up and swallow me.* Yet this move toward isolation becomes the very fuel that keeps the secrecy and shame alive. The more isolated we are, the more ashamed we get, and the greater the secrecy of our emotions becomes. Feelings become divided into good and bad, wanted and unwanted. An emotional hierarchy is perpetuated.

"Sounds like you felt ashamed for eating that cookie," I observed. Kathleen's face reddened.

"This is so familiar," she said. "Growing up, I was always made to feel wrong for eating or feeling pleasure."

Kathleen's statement is a good example of how an internal view—in this case, deep shame—was deeply influenced by negative messages from her family. Appreciate for a moment how we live day in and day out with the messages received from our families and the environment in which we live. All of us are shaped by what we believe we are. With mindfulness, we become aware of how these messages resurface. We meet them, this time in the form of uncomfortable sensations, distracting thoughts, or irritating feelings.

Shame is one of the most challenging emotions we have to deal with. It gives us the primal urge to withdraw from connection, because it was connection that threatened us in the first place.

Try this:

Meet shame by gently moving toward it. Own your shame; be fearless; look it in the eye. Say to yourself, *Here it is, let it be bright, hot, sticky, or ugly*—the thing you least want. By noticing shame and letting it be, it will bring you back into connection. The very moment you can turn toward it, shame loses its grip. It moves on and you will notice that it was hot and unpleasant and connected with past interpretations, but nothing more. After the shame moment has passed, you can reflect on what the shame has to teach you. What is the message here? If the shame is an intelligent expression, what does it have to say right now?

Anger: The Truth-Teller

There is a well-known story of the Buddha visiting a nobleman who became angry and unleashed his aggression on his guest in an angry tirade. The Buddha paused and asked the nobleman how he usually received people. The nobleman answered that he fed them and gave them wine. "What if they refused the food and drink?" asked the Buddha. "Who would that belong to?" The nobleman answered that it would still be his food. The Buddha replied that he would not accept the nobleman's anger and slander and that the nobleman would have to sit with his own anger. "That," said the Buddha, "still belongs to you."

With anger, we want to unload the feeling, express our agitation right away, push it on to someone else, or give someone a "piece of our mind." We seldom wait to express and consider the consequences. In the story, the Buddha was trying to teach the nobleman that anger was the nobleman's responsibility and that he would still be stuck with it if the Buddha refused to accept it. When we can mindfully observe anger (in ourselves or others), we can interrupt the automatic need to unload it. First, consider anger's helpful message. What can be good about anger, you might ask? Anger in its purest form is a powerful energy, the direct and hot expression of dissent. It's a *no*, a boundary—not the corrupt version in which it is violently acted out as an expression of abuse or out-of-control rage. What gets confusing is when anger as an intelligent sensation gets mixed up with the justification to act it out. Where we get caught is when we fuel it, justify it, ruminate over it, or take it personally. We can get lost in the aftermath of its intensity and lose touch with its righteous message. Few of us are coached to feel anger as just a hot emotion with a direct message or simple truth.

To be clear, I am not advocating that you act out anger; rather, I am advocating that you *feel* anger but *not* act it out. It's a two-step process, similar to what I taught my son's third-grade class: Notice, feel it, cool it, and then respond. The more you can practice anger and *have* it, the more you can learn to harness this powerful emotion and not feel the need to react.

Try this:

   In a moment of anger, yours or someone else's, ask these questions: *What is the truth behind this anger? If this anger could speak, what would it say? What would be help to calm this intensity right now? What are its physical manifestations? How long does it take for me to think calmly after the anger comes up? If the anger is aimed at me, does it carry a message that is important for me to hear?*

Sadness and Grief: The Quiet Messengers

By their very nature, sadness and grief offer an opportunity to practice mindfulness, because when we feel these emotions we are more inclined to slow down and be reflective. In one 2010 study, researchers examined the neural mapping of sadness and discovered positive effects of mindfulness. The more subjects were able to notice bodily sensations associated with the sadness, the more they were able to create emotional balance. Decreased depression scores indicated that mindful body awareness helps to lessen sadness (Farb & Anderson, 2010).

Sometimes you may not be able to avoid feeling your sadness, which can help you appreciate the fragility of life and how fleeting your moments of true happiness are. Life is short and impermanent. You can feel sad about what has been lost and treat yourself and others more gently.

I consider sadness and grief to exist on a spectrum. Grief is a deeper, more lasting stage of sadness, often following a deep loss or trauma. You may be quick to want to move on or "feel better," and you may think you have little stamina to stay with the gray shades of life. However, try staying quietly with your emotions and notice your tendency to want to "get out." A time of grieving can also be healing. It's where your body and mind rest and integrate and digest what has happened. Value its darkness. Sitting quietly with grief or sadness can lessen the intensity.

Try this:
If sadness and grief are part of your emotional landscape, allow yourself time to feel them in your body. You may need not just a few minutes or hours, but quality time where you track what is truly happening. What does the sadness feel like in your body? Where do you notice grief? What happens when you practice mindfulness and welcome the emotions? What is your expe-
(continues)

rience as you let the textures of sadness be and not try to change them? Can you trust grief to have its time? These questions can help you let these emotions be as you sit with them. And remember, these emotions won't last.

Fear and Anxiety: Helping You Survive

Fear and anxiety are strong biological survival factors. When they get triggered, your responses may be quite primal. Fear is your direct biological response to a known threat. Anxiety, however, can pervade your whole being in a more vague, nonspecific way. Fear and anxiety also exist on a spectrum. The instinctual nature of fear urges you to protect yourself or flee, while anxiety diverts your energy toward being hyperalert and always on the lookout for a threat. Both can hold you in their grip. The challenge is to get acquainted with fear or anxiety, and just as with shame, look it straight in the eye. Allow yourself to feel the trembling or agitation inside, and notice how it takes over your thinking mind. The goal here is to develop the stamina to stay with your bodily sensations without buying into the drama of them.

In a famous teaching story, a woman is running away from a tiger. As she fights to escape, she is in such a panic she doesn't bother to stop and look. She can feel the huge claws and the large, frightening teeth that will surely grasp her. But, out of the corner of her eye, she sees there is suddenly no motion behind her. She looks again and realizes that the object of her fear was a paper tiger, gently rippling in the wind.

This is the tricky business of fear and anxiety. The paper tigers of our mind are usually what make us run, but when we can face what is, there may still be a tiger, but the magnitude of the threat is usually much smaller than we thought.

Bringing a present, centered focus to fearful and anxious moments is crucial. Remind yourself that fear is present but that no danger is happening. Say to yourself, *I am learning to meet this fear [or this anxiety] gradually and safely.* Both fear and anxiety become dominant emotional states when we are in the midst of them. They place our thinking in the past or future but not in the present. Practicing mindfulness is very important, as it will bring you back and remind you of another reality, the one here and now and the one in which you have awareness of and power over your choices.

Making room for these emotions is about regulating your emotional state back into a realm of manageability. You can deal with doses of fear and anxiety, but it's hard to deal with being overwhelmed. Let the fear and anxiety be there in small doses. It's okay to walk around, take breaks, and renew your resources many times if needed. Recognizing your anxiety and taking action toward your improved well-being will change the difficult state into a manageable state. Get creative: Try a walking meditation in nature instead of sitting. One of my clients, for example, could manage her anxiety mindfully only when she was near a body of water. She would swim and breathe gently and feel into her body. This would help her regulate the intensity of her anxiety. There are many ways to be mindful. It's okay to find a healthful activity that is calming and soothing. After that, it's easier to inquire into the nature of your anxiety or fear. Treat yourself kindly when you sit quietly and inquire into these emotions. What do your fear and anxiety tell you? You don't want to know the story of what happened or will happen, but what are they saying right now?

Try this:

Learn to distinguish fear caused by truly dangerous situations from fear that is embellished by past interpretations. Sitting quietly with the intensity can help here. Come back to the body again and again and notice the details of your anxiety or fear. What is the quality of this feeling? What impulses go with the feeling of fear? What do you notice in your body? Where is your

(continues)

breath? Feel the urge to run, hide, fight, or freeze. Let that be, and breathe calmly into it. Notice how it's not true right now.

Allow yourself to feel the fear or anxiety in small doses. Give yourself a break by going for a walk, moving your body, or reminding yourself, *I am learning to meet this fear [or this anxiety] gradually and safely.*

Joy: Appreciating the Moment

Joy is as important as any of the strong emotions discussed above. We tend to wish for happiness, but when it's there we have a hard time taking it in. We yearn to be happy and then lament when the feeling is gone. What we miss is the appreciation of happiness when it's right here. The preciousness of happiness and how fleeting it can be is a reminder that all emotions are truly fleeting and impermanent. Nothing lasts. We need to celebrate what is and not dwell on what has gone before and what is to come. Often when I lead a meditation and my students experience happy feelings, they are quick to get up and change course rather than sitting with those feelings, as if they need to spend what they have just gained. How about lingering and cherishing the happy feeling instead?

Because we may have a negative bias, we may brush aside joy or happiness, minimizing it or moving on quickly without actually savoring what is. Joy, I have noticed, can sometimes trigger sadness about the past, feelings of loss, or worry about the future. This is part of what is called the cycle of suffering. We constantly are on the run from our emotions. We fear and anticipate and long and grieve for other times. The only way through is to accept all emotions as they are and appreciate their wise aspects. Let go of making joy and happiness the ultimate goal; rather, enjoy all the various textures of life as they are. Think of a painting with a wide array of colors and hues. Let it be as it was in the process of creation—wild and messy and unpredictable.

Try this:

Try taking in joy by hanging out with it when it comes. How long does it take to worry that it might leave again? Can you rest in not being able to control all aspects of your life? Can you trust that emotions come and go and are as hues of color to be noticed, expressed, or felt as they are, without judgment? Can you sit still when joy comes and feel all of it? Can you rest in the goodness of whatever arises? You might have the unexpected surprise of a joyful moment. Linger there by slowing down and savoring it. This can be a spectacular sunset you happen to catch, or a moment of spontaneous laughter with a stranger. Harvest that moment by giving it all of your attention.

Exercise: Loud and Clear:
The Courage to Face What Is

20–30 minutes

This exercise combines facing what is and creating new perspectives. When you name for yourself the challenges you face, they become more manageable. This is a practice that will take a while to settle into. It's not easy to face what is. Watch for the tendency to explain, fix, avoid, and defend. The challenge here is to drop all of these attempts and just be patient with what is.

To prepare yourself, make sure you have a piece of paper and a pen. This is a "scribble and sit" technique (a little sitting, a little scribbling, until the layers of the story are peeled away). Pay attention to what's in the way and use the scribble technique to move these "voices" out of the way. Give yourself creative license: You can scribble all over the paper; no straight lines are required, and this doesn't have to be a list. You will write about the issue you face; then you will sit for a short while and notice your body. Then you will take another issue, or a different angle on the same issue, and write about that.

1. Set the Right Frame

- Keep a pen and paper close by.
- Establish a good sitting posture by making sure that your shoulders are aligned with your pelvis and that your neck is resting easily without any tension. Slightly tuck in your chin so the back of your spine is more upright.
- Assume a relaxed-alert posture. Rest your hands on your thighs or knees.
- Reconnect with your breath and follow the steady in-and-out of your inhale and exhale.
- Settle your thoughts by labeling them and letting them go.
- Allow yourself to get quiet.

2. Stay and Study

- Bring up the emotion or issue you are dealing with or are curious to explore. You might need some time to feel into its various qualities. You can use the earlier exercise on scanning emotions (p. 101) to sense the textures and details of the story.
- Contemplate the story for a moment. Get detailed. Notice the familiar story line: "He did . . . I did . . . they did . . . I always . . . she never . . ."
- Now turn to your "scribble and sit" technique. Write down the familiar story line ("She always . . ."). Then pause your pen and return to the "sitting" portion of the exercise again.
- Turn your attention inside and get quiet. Sense your body. Do you feel stirred up? Calmer?
- Call up the next layer of this memory or feeling. What is here now? Sadness? Anger? Numbness? Irritation?
- "Scribble and sit" again. Write down the next feelings. Remember that you can write randomly in bits and pieces.
- Pause your pen and sit quietly. What is here now? What has changed?
- Keep writing until the urge to scribble wanes. There may be a natural ending here.
- Sit quietly for five minutes and see what comes up. Is it quieter inside you? What are your emotions like now?

- How does it feel now to "meet" the unpleasant feeling or issue?
- Check back in with your body. See if you can return to the posture or if it has changed. Soften your breath and any tension you might feel.
- Be open and pay close attention to the effects the "scribble and sit" technique has on your memory recall.

3. Anchor and Harvest

- You can finish by writing if you like.
- Most importantly, reflect on whether you were able to find calm in the midst of this challenge.
- Be patient. It may take a few times before you're able to work with the very heart of your emotion or issue.
- Return to this practice many times if you like.

Everyday Mindfulness Tip

Massage your temples, feet, or scalp. Take a long bath in a tub or Jacuzzi. Drink a glass of water. Cuddle with your pet or your beloved. Go for a long, slow walk. Curl up in your bed during the day for a short rest. Take time to indulge your senses. Allow yourself to have mindful body experiences that enhance pleasure and well-being. Can you take it in? Can you sense the softness of a touch, the release of pressure, the temperature of water or air, your relaxed breathing, or the warmth of another person? What is that like in your sensate body? See if you can deliberately take in the pleasure of this moment and stay present. Allow your sensations to dominate. Give your thoughts a break.

KEY 6

RIDE THROUGH TOUGH TIMES

Success and failure are your journey.   —CHÖGYAM TRUNGPA

"Look around you," the soft-spoken mother of four said to me. "People are having a hard time. Stress is everywhere." She knew what she was talking about. Her husband had been laid off two years before and her family had struggled to make ends meet. This proud Ivy League graduate was ashamed to admit she had used food stamps to feed her children. She became teary-eyed as she spoke.

"How did you get through it?" I asked.

"I don't know," she said. "I didn't really. I just survived. I went kind of numb. I took one day at a time. All I could do was deal with what was in front of me. We made it; we are okay for now."

When times are tough, you, like my client, may simply want to cope, escape, grind through, or make the difficulty go away. The last thing you may want to do is be mindful about your difficulties. Yet this is the very moment when you can count on your inner witness to bring moments of sanity and peace.

Some stress is normal, and you are well equipped to deal with it when you can rest and rejuvenate. Your capacity to endure, get creative, or move quickly through a highly intense time in your life can be rewarding and build inner confidence. When you can meet a job loss with a fighting attitude and find new possibilities, you may uncover strengths you never knew you had. Or when you can accept a relationship breakup with patience and kindness toward yourself, you may find a new way to be in the world. When stress overwhelms your normal coping response, however, you may crumble into defeat, depression, or loss of perspective. The intensity can take you off guard, and you may want to go into protection mode—that is, to put up your defenses or retreat when you perceive danger. The body's natural responses to perceived threat are instinctual, but if this initial shock wears off and the self-protective stance is still there, you are now dealing with emotional numbing and avoidance that can be more harmful than protective. This type of defense is effective as a short-term reaction until the threat has subsided, but it is never meant to be long-term. When stressors, real or perceived, become chronic, the body responds and resets its threshold to a new level of intensity. You might not recognize how stressed you are on a daily basis and may assume you're just as stressed as everyone else. Your body can't keep up, and over time will show the effects in physical, emotional, or mental imbalances.

Some people thrive in spite of ongoing stressors. Why they seem to grow under adversity and others falter is not easy to understand. I have learned through my clients that triumphing over difficulties (and not just surviving) is a complex and multilayered process. It's not just about having a good attitude, adequate help, good resources, or intellectual understanding. It has to do with being mindful of yourself and your body. Consider these questions: Are you aware of how you regulate your stress? Can you rest or rejuvenate even during challenging times? Do you know how to find internal comfort and strength?

Key 6 will help you learn to do exactly this: bring down the levels of anxiety, fear, and stress during tough times. This is a fundamental life skill everyone should be taught, but unfortunately our culture endorses instant escape or ready-made responses to the detriment of our mental and physical health. An average of just 20 minutes a day can change the brain's responses to stress, boost memory function, and reduce gray matter density in the area of the brain associated with stress and anxiety. In one study (Brown & Kirk, 2003), a mindfulness scale was used to measure the ability of cancer patients to focus their attention on the positive aspects of their lives rather than being consumed by negative thoughts. The researchers found that mindfulness increased positive emotional states in these patients by helping them to become more aware of their unconscious processes and thus to execute more cognitive control.

Actively engaging with mindfulness allows you to shape your experience rather than being a passive bystander in your life. This ability is crucial when you are dealing with the challenges life can throw at you. You might prefer to shut down, go on autopilot, revert to earlier coping mechanisms, or get trapped in negative thought patterns. When you recognize that you can change how you relate to a situation and actively participate in that process, you may gain motivation, support, and strength.

During tough times, it's easy to lose perspective and get lost in the worry, stress, and anxiety of it all. However, there is also an upside: You can discover new perspectives on what is important. This gives you opportunities to practice kindness and tenderness toward yourself and others. You can use mindfulness to help balance the stress and find little islands of calm in a time when your heart is most vulnerable. Rather than shutting down and becoming bitter or resentful, you can allow this tenderness to be part of your experience and make way for new possibilities. Tough times happen, but they can also facilitate transformation. Quite often, this may be the kind of change you yearn for, even if you never bargained on it arriving in this way.

A Word of Caution

Since this chapter addresses the darker, more challenging emotions that can come with tough times, it's important to distinguish between having gloomy moments and being chronically depressed. There's a significant difference between going through a patch of emotional darkness that can be worked with and experiencing depression that needs professional treatment. The exercises in this chapter are designed to help you through difficult times by calming the anxiety and fear that accompanies them. Moments of darkness and even mild despair are normal when you recover painful emotions and begin to address hurts from the past. A "normal" course is for the dark moments to ease and subside. You may experience new insights or feel better after touching into long-lost feelings. After the gloom, there is brightness and understanding, and a sense of hope returns.

If you are having one of these tough spots and are willing to explore it on your own, then the exercises in this chapter might serve you. Usually, when clients can meet these moments, they lift and change. If this happens to you, this will serve as an indicator that the exercises are an appropriate course of action for you. However, if your darkness persists and does not change after mindful sitting and attempts to do the exercises, or if you notice that you are not able to function as you used to, please consult a professional. Being impaired in your relationships and in your daily life are both warning signs that you may be clinically depressed or suffering from the effects of trauma. Either requires outside help. Severe depression can be debilitating and require professional intervention. Some traumas need to be addressed by the gentle, empathetic care of a therapist, because the pain may feel too overwhelming. You may be experiencing the effects of a trauma or depression that you can't get over by yourself, and it's essential to have another caring person (preferably a professional) listen and understand. In all cases, please be gentle with yourself.

Remember Your Resources

When stress is high and life feels unbalanced, it's important to call upon your resources. These might include a loving family, a good friend, a positive attitude toward life, a supportive church community, or a healthy body. Resources can also be mental, emotional, and spiritual associations of a neutral or positive nature that you already have or may be developing; for example, the love you have for your pet, the exhilaration you feel when you take a long hike in nature, and the confidence you gain from improving at something important or challenging to you are all resources. In this book, I suggest using resources that you are familiar with and that have helped you in the past, such as your faith, the support of a loved one, or the thought of someone who believes in you.

Resources offer emotional stability, calm, or a much-needed reprieve. We can think of them as refuge from a brewing storm or shelter from the emotional ups and downs of life. Under Key 4, I suggested you feel the Earth underneath you (p. 90), so please return to that exercise as needed. Additionally, in this chapter, I am suggesting the element of Sky as a resource to stabilize you during tough times (p. 152). The Earth is a stable ground on which you can walk, sit, or lie, and which carries you and nourishes your body. The Sky is vast, open, and spacious and can open new horizons of thought and perspective. Consider your associations with these elements and determine whether their support can be added to your resource repertoire. If these elements don't work for you and you have others that better suit you, please substitute them as needed. The main point is to find something neutral and bigger than you than you can rest in and trust, so that it counterbalances any upheaval you are working with. The freer this entity is from negative associations, the better.

Let's begin by considering the many resources you already possess. In the following exercise, I ask you to sit quietly and reflect on strengths you have relied on in the past to help you make it through. You will then write about how you have managed this. Throughout the exercise, focus on your inner strengths as well as how your body feels. For example, you might notice a moment of relaxation, a clear mind, or a sense of peace.

Exercise: Strength Inventory

 *10 minutes*

Part of your mindfulness journey is to remember the inner resources you already possess and what you can further develop in your repertoire. In this exercise, remember to pause frequently and tune back in to your body, and then write some more. Stay away from generalizations and focus on what has helped you with outlook, motivation, or inspiration during challenging periods of your life.

1. Set the Right Frame
- Find a comfortable sitting position. Close your eyes.
- Direct your focus to your breath and body. Remember to slow down and let your body and mind settle. Remind yourself to sit relaxed and alert, checking your postural habits and gently correcting them.
- Take your time. See if you can settle your thoughts.

2. Stay and Study
- Remember a time when you experienced a serious challenge. Recall how it felt in your body by remembering the details. You can visualize the place or people you were with to help you recall this time.
- How did you discover strength at that time? Is there a place in your body where you felt strong and connected with yourself? Feel into your belly, heart, and legs. These are places where people typically find inner strength, so check to see if that was true for you. Was there an overall sense of strength, and did it have energy and persistence? See how you relate to this idea of finding strength inside of you.
- Reflect on the following in your writing: *Looking at my life so*

*far, what has been the most challenging time? What did I learn
at these intense moments about myself? What inner resources,
creativity, or strengths did I discover that I did not previously
know I had?* Let an image or memory emerge. *How did my
body help me in those times? What has been a safe place in my
body to rely on?*

- Don't analyze or embellish; just see what comes up.
- As you write, pause every now and then and check in with
  your mindfulness. What is your experience as you recall these
  moments?
- Let the writing come from whatever emerges.

3. Anchor and Harvest

- Finish reading this chapter, then return to your writing and
  note what came up for you as you read the chapter.
- Did you uncover new resources or moments of strength?

Coping Strategies: Numbing and Escaping

A common response to stress is to "get through" by numbing out or
not being present with the pain and suffering, which are sometimes too much to bear. It is understandable that we are pain-
avoidant—our bodies and minds are hardwired to avoid unpleasant
circumstances. However, this is often not the best choice, for when
we get overwhelmed, we revert to coping strategies we have learned
by default or example. These coping strategies may have worked
once or twice but do not provide lasting resolution. We end up
more depressed, more unhappy, or stuck in old habits.

Numbing can take the form of entertaining ourselves with
social media, TV, video games, or mindless activities that take us
away for a while or help us forget the worries and lose ourselves in
the numbness. We can also escape through drugs, alcohol, food,
or any substance or behavior that eases the unpleasant feelings.
Jenny, a young client addicted to prescription drugs, once told me
that she hated taking them and dreaded the thought of using them.

"I go on autopilot," she said, "One minute I am telling myself, 'I should not be using; it's bad for me.' The next moment I am there, blissing out, forgetting everything. But I don't know what happened in between. I kind of just numbed out; I can't even remember how I got there."

Numbing is a response to a pain threshold reached inside. We can't tolerate it anymore and will do anything to make our current feelings go away. We become mindless and fall prey to habits and rationalizations. Shame, guilt, and remorse often follow the numbing, but these also fuel the need to go numb. A cycle of self-loathing sets in as well as a tendency to avoid tolerating difficult feelings. Jenny initially didn't see the point when I guided her to pay attention to them: "What good are the feelings when they make me feel so crappy?"

Witnessing a friend or client in despair and distress can be tough for anyone. Even a friend or therapist can be overwhelmed by the magnitude of the suffering. And if we say to someone like Jenny, "Just hang in there," or "Stay with it and be curious—it will soon subside," this might feel defeating to the one who is suffering, like a mountain too difficult to climb. However, being genuinely empathic can help the client or friend soften to his or her pain. With Jenny, for instance, I said, "Wow. This is so hard. It's just too much. Of course you want to numb out and not deal with it all. You are hurting." In that moment, Jenny felt heard. The deeply frightened part of her began to relax and get curious about her experience.

Jenny could not be with her pain in an open way when she was anxious and tight, but she could begin to soften when she felt understood. Like Jenny, most of my clients already know what they need to do, and they know when their behavior is destructive. What they don't know is how to be met with empathy and kindness. As soon as they realize someone "gets" them, a natural state of curiosity and kindness opens up.

While you may not always have a therapist at hand to listen during difficult times, you do have mindfulness available at all moments. Just as you have been learning in previous chapters, remember to slow down, give yourself a time-out, sit down, and breathe into your body. Remember that you do have a kind and intelligent body, even if it hurts at this moment. Although these actions can feel like small kindnesses in a sea of pain, they do help. They can help you find your way to safety. In these tough moments, you will soften, open to what is real, and meet yourself. Yes, it may be painful, overwhelming, or too much, but it is real and right now. You are stronger than you know and you have resources. You can build resources as you work with the moments where you just want to go numb. The very fact that you turn toward what scares you builds inner resilience. One moment at a time, you can learn to see what to do or who to reach out to for help. In this unexpected way, your pain can guide you toward getting the help you need.

Try this:

When numbness comes into your awareness, reach out to someone. Talk to a friend, call your trusted parent or mentor, or simply connect with a stranger in line at the grocery store. Often you need human contact and connection or stimulation and a slight shift of perspective when you get caught in the zone of numbness. Make an effort to talk to your neighbor as she brings in the garbage can, or give a lending hand when you see someone struggling to open the door. Reach out and connect. We are mammals, and we thrive when we connect with other mammals. I have been surprised at how uplifted I feel just by walking my dog and stopping to talk to other dog owners as my dog greets and sniffs theirs. We are no different. Sometimes we need others to jolt us out of our bubble and spark our curiosity.

Getting Unstuck

Andrea was having an anxious night. She couldn't stop her mind from continually rehashing the details of her husband's words to

her right before he left, confirming her suspicions of the affair she
had long suspected. As Andrea tossed and turned in her empty
bed, she went over and over the details of their last encounter. Self-
doubt and anxiety about her financial future and the elderly
mother she was caring for all kept her awake.

Each decision and turning point of the last twenty years of marriage came to the surface during that night. She now regretted that
she had never finished getting her medical license, but she hadn't
needed it after she met Mark, a successful surgeon who said he
would provide for her. She had settled into her routine as a busy
wife, caring for their household and, later, her ailing mother. Mark's
affair had taken her completely by surprise. Andrea's chronic fatigue
had been puzzling to her physician, but that night as her thoughts
went in circles, she realized how she hadn't wanted to see the truth
of her life. The slow emotional numbing that had set into place
years earlier had been brushed aside as temporary nuisances. She
had not listened to the bodily symptoms of fatigue and exhaustion.

Not only was Andrea overcome with grief that night, but she
also felt a crushing fear of the future. However, at that moment,
she also had a new experience—of the truth. Like the missing
piece of a puzzle, she noticed that her dread of the future was
fueled by the low energy and creeping fear she had felt throughout
the course of her marriage. Mark's confidence and protective
nature had initially served as a cozy nest for her low self-esteem. It
was as if she had fallen into a sweet slumber of forgetfulness. Life
had seemed good and fine, but it was not authentic and vibrant.

In one of our therapy sessions, Andrea called this state of mind
"my sleeping beauty." It had been too much to face the pain. She
had been vehemently against feeling anything that was not beautiful, easy, or light and had avoided any emotions that were remotely
painful. That night, however, when the pain came crashing down,
she could avoid it no longer. She sat up and got quiet. Memories
flooded her mind. She resolved to settle in and listen to whatever
would come. "I think I found your mindfulness," she said to me,
half smiling, the next morning. "It kind of just happened. I had
nothing else to run from. I just had to become still. I sat there in

my bed, ready to either go crazy or go quiet. The weight in my chest was so oppressive I could barely breathe. But I remembered that you told me I could just be with one moment at a time, and then another and yet another. I didn't have to comprehend all the moments. Just one."

"And did it help you?" I asked hesitantly.

"Yes," she answered. "At first it was really hard, but then I just felt my body, my breath, and it got very simple. The pain eased some. I cried a lot, but I didn't feel so crushed anymore. There was a way through, one mini-moment at a time."

Getting unstuck takes courage. It means facing what is, ruthlessly and without fear. Even if this happens only for mini-moments, it's a start. You are looking fear right in the face. It's a paradox to be frightened yet meet the fear. You look at it and stay with it, just as Andrea did. We've all had moments when we've reached the end of a long road, and we have a decision to make. The moment we become fearless is the moment we get unstuck.

When you can sit down and face the gloom and sit with the truth of a situation, a shift can occur. It may not be conceivable at the moment of darkness. The anticipation and fear of what is to come can be so huge and overwhelming that it's hard to think of an alternative. It may feel counterintuitive to stop and face it. All you want to do is run, hide, or scream. But the very best medicine is to stop, face, and listen. When you build a relationship with fear itself, it loses its powerful grip on your body and mind.

Try this:

When you find yourself having a dark moment, don't try to fix or understand the darkness. Return to your posture, sit upright, gently straighten, drop your shoulders, and lift through your spine. Just be with your body, one mini-moment at a time. Lift the corners of your mouth and smile. Pay attention to what is happening as you shift your posture and face slightly. According to research, shifting your posture and smiling can make you feel more confident and happy right away (Briñol, Petty, & Wagner, 2009; Strack, Martin, & Stepper,1988). Try assuming a queenly or kingly posture. See what happens to your mood.

Getting Unstuck, Part Two

Andrea's healing began the night she discovered a quiet place in the midst of the pain—but this was a starting point, not the end. There were many weeks and months where the pain and "stuckness" of her situation felt like too much to bear. At times she numbed out, or had despairing moments where she pretended nothing had happened. Many times she would come in to see me and report that she felt even more stuck than before. I encouraged her to be mindful of not just the mini-moments but the life stage she was in. For Andrea, suddenly becoming a single, divorced parent at age forty-eight was not easy. She was not only facing her sadness over the breakup but also her fears of aging and being without a partner. She had the tools to pursue her healing, and at times she used them, but at other times she forgot to be mindful. It's important to remember that you are a naturally "mindful" human being, but your emotions, life story, and current stressors can mask the natural state of your mind and body. Andrea's mindful exploration into her feelings, imaginings, narratives, and fears, one mini-moment at a time, made the overwhelming anticipation for the future more manageable. She began to face each moment as it came, grounding herself and reminding herself to return to the present. Over time, this practical application gave her more confidence to adopt a positive outlook.

There is a lovely experiment a meditation teacher I once knew created and taught. She called it "mind in the jar." A big glass bowl filled with water sits on a table. Small jars with different-colored sand are then carefully arranged in front of the glass bowl. The participants gather round and get quiet as they reflect on the feelings they are having in the moment. One by one, each person steps forward and takes a pinch of whichever color of sand represents his or her feelings: blue for a moody day, bright red for happiness, soft pink for love, iridescent white for clarity. One by one, everyone places their pinch of colored sand on the water's surface.

Once everyone has spoken their feelings and sprinkled the sand into the bowl, the teacher takes a big wooden spoon and swirls the water and the sand, explaining how speediness and stress mix up our minds and bodies and how our feelings all mix together. She suddenly takes out the spoon, and the water twirls around in a tornado formation. As the participants watch the spectacle, the movement of the water slows and the sparkling grains of sand descend to the bottom of the bowl. The muddy mess separates into a dense layer of sand on the bottom of the jar and calm waters above. The water becomes clear and still. Just like your mind.

Once you stop and notice, a clarity returns that is akin to your natural mind state. The swirling sand grains (emotions) are temporary, even if at the time they feel all important, all engulfing. You may place a lot of emphasis on the crisis, feeling, or event of the moment and less on remembering that you "are" mindful if you care to pause and inquire. The moment you pay attention and stop, you can feel, sense, and know the natural state of who you really are.

Andrea took a full year to begin to find herself again and an additional four years to fully recover from the shock and upheaval of the changes her messy divorce brought. Finding peacefulness, calmness, and curiosity take time—one mini-moment at a time, in fact. Have patience and try again, and again. Becoming mindful is not a final "resting place" to achieve but a way to be in your life: more awake, more in touch with what matters, and above all more curious about what is in this present moment right now.

Caught in Old Patterns: Addicted to Intensity

When Rick, the young veteran described under Key 3, first came into my office, he wanted to find out why he was so full of fear and how he could live "a more liberated life," as he put it. He'd had an uneventful upbringing in the suburbs and had been close to his family and friends as a child. His years of serving in the armed forces had left an imprint on his psyche and body. He described his life as "a yo-yo." During the week, he was flat and listless, waking midday and barely getting out of the house. His social world was confined to a few friends, and he was now a solemn twenty-nine-year old living off his savings. His face was sunken with hints of depression. He withheld eye contact as if he was afraid to meet the world.

During the weekend, a whole other persona emerged and his time was filled with high-speed activities such as bungee jumping, race car driving, and skydiving. At night he would go out clubbing until the early morning and use drugs to enhance his amped-up state. He would barely sleep. The weekends became a blur and the week felt long and agonizing until the weekend came around. He was "addicted to intensity," as he put it, and his weekends were "alive" and his weekdays "boring." Not only was Rick suffering from the effects of addiction and trauma, as it turned out, but he was also confusing intensity with aliveness. He needed this kind of high drama and intensity to feel alive.

The bodily depression and withdrawal symptoms made his experience even more excruciating. He kept repeating this cycle week after week, until he began to recognize that something wasn't working. The initial high of the weekends became flatter, his depression on Mondays because darker, and his overall health began to decline. He was at a loss. Rick's reason for coming to therapy was to find a way to enliven the intensity of his life; instead, I offered him mindfulness exercises, or what he called "meditations where I watch the paint dry." His brain and body were so entrenched in a cycle of addiction that he couldn't stand getting calm or quiet. Every time he approached silence, he became agitated and wanted to escape. Slowing down and listening to his internal self felt almost painful.

Rick was confusing the search for the "highs" with "intensity," but intensity is not necessarily aliveness. If intensity is what you're craving, then it might be helpful to ask yourself, *What part of me is not alive? What part of me desires to be more vibrant?* Rick had gotten lost in his trauma symptoms and addictive behavior. He was trying to get out of it, but his means were flawed. He had not learned that intensity needed to be stabilized and resourced through his body. He had not faced some of his fears in a calm way and was trying to wrestle danger into submission in order to find some peace. He struck me as a young and brave man who was tackling a lion over and over again but not realizing that he could just look at the lion and didn't need to fight it.

Any time you face hard times, you need an anchor. There is no need to tackle hardship with an attitude of aggression and self-destructiveness. You can learn to inch your way to the face-off, and you can accumulate some help along the way. Learning how to ground the body through gentle awareness stabilizes the wildness of the mind. Consider this the eddy of the river, where you can take a break before the next section of white water. You need to pace yourself. The journey is intense enough; you don't need to add more to it. If you can learn from Rick's example, you can better pace the intensity so you can actually see what is needed. In a reactionary, addicted-to-intensity mode, you might think you're facing things head on and not even be able to see that you're thrashing in troubled waters.

Exercise: Getting Unstuck

 *25 minutes*

This is a writing exercise to help you reflect on the places in your life where you are stuck. You will identify the hurdles you face by answering questions. The idea is to find liberation from the blockages by connecting to what is underneath. I suggest that you read one question at a time and then answer it right away without editing. Keep writing until you have nothing else to say and then go on to the next question. It's important that you don't edit, revise, or proofread your writing, as you will get more stuck if you apply judgment.

1. Set the Right Frame

Set the intention to work with the theme of "stuckness." Allow a few moments to rest your mind and body. You can lie down and breathe into your belly and chest to empty your thoughts. Simply stay with your body awareness and pay attention to the present moment. Then sit up slowly and take another moment before you engage in the writing.

I recommend that you slow down while you write; move the pen a little slower than usual. Every now and then, remember to take a deliberate breath. Tune in to your body each time you sit with a new question. See if you can let the answers and writing come to you, let go of the stories, and see what wants to be written. This is as much a reflection exercise as it is a mindful writing exploration. Trust what comes out of you and onto the paper.

2. Stay and Study

Reflect on these questions one at a time:

- Where in your body do you feel stuck? What sensations go with the feeling of being stuck?
- If the sensation in your body had an image or color, what would it be?
- What are the stories you tell yourself about stuckness? Recall some moments where you felt stuck or unable to make an important decision. Perhaps you were unable to move to another apartment, or maybe you weren't accepted into the college you hoped to intend? What do you remember about these times? Did you have recurring thoughts or feelings? What did you think and feel about this stuck place? What messages did you receive from others about the situation?
- Go to the broader sense of stuckness. If you think of stuckness as a feeling in your body, where would you locate it? How would you describe it? What does it mean to be stuck?

- As you are writing and feeling into this theme, are you aware of your breath? Does anything interesting come up as you reflect on this topic right now?
- Where would the opposite of "stuck" live in your body? What do you imagine it would feel like in your body to not be stuck?
- What do you think can you help get there?

3. Anchor and Harvest

After writing, take time to sit quietly and, without any particular focus in your meditation, be open to the present moment of what is. Once you identify the stuck places, it is easier to sit and track what is coming up. Chances are, your thinking mind will get clearer, so be patient and wait for it. See if you are experiencing curiosity toward what has been revealed. Can you apply some kindness toward the stuck places you have been through? You will further explore the importance of self-kindness and self-compassion under Key 8. Having a gentle attitude toward once-stuck places is a great first step in practicing self-kindness. If that doesn't happen, try again at another time. If you can't feel kindness or clarity, don't give up. This is okay. Try again later and get curious about what *is* coming up. When you are busy being stuck, your thinking mind can take over and get in the way of your being open to any exercise. Remember that this is an ongoing practice, and you may need to learn just how mindless and not present you are before you can change.

Going Deeper: Discovering Hidden Strength in Dark Moments

Wendy's cancer had been in remission for five years, so it came as a shock when she felt several strange lumps in her breast tissue one morning. She didn't want to go through it all over again: the endless doctor visits and the intrusion into her body. She felt traumatized just thinking about her ordeal with cancer. Wendy felt betrayed by her body, and once again she was faced with tough choices. Her mood changed dramatically. This vibrant, optimistic musician became severely depressed. Soon she stopped composing and playing music and quit her job as a music teacher. When she came to me, she was convinced that death was on her doorstep, and she refused to have her lumps checked. "What's the use?" she said, "I cheated death once. I can't do it twice."

Months went by, and the urgings of her partner and children to get medical attention fell on deaf ears. She isolated herself and her relationships deteriorated. She fell into a dark and lonely place. Fear gripped her completely. In addition to refusing medical help, she didn't want to continue therapy or her meditation practice. She had resigned herself to quitting. This was a stark development, and it was challenging to reach her. To her credit, she did continue the weekly therapy, even though she had all but given up. I was facing a difficult patch myself, as I was uncertain how to help her in this "given-up" place.

In one therapy session, as an aside, she mentioned that she had a lot of "unfinished business." I inquired. One piece was a FedEx box that had been sitting in her closet for the past ten years. It contained the ashes of her beloved father. Every time she saw the box, she felt guilty for not having conducted a proper ceremony to release his ashes. I gently mentioned that it might be time to do so, because what would become of them if she got too sick? She was startled by that thought. "What do you suggest?" she asked.

"Well, maybe it's time to face your father's passing and give the ashes a final resting place." Wendy started to tear up.

"I know exactly what he would have wanted. He would have liked to listen to some calming music and see the ocean one last time."

The following week, Wendy came back into the office with a very different demeanor. She appeared lighter and reported to me that she had done a private ceremony for her father. She recounted how she had gone to the ocean, unpacked her flute, and composed a music piece for him on the spot. As she released the ashes into the ocean waves, she said through a stream of tears, "To last a life-time." Then she told me, "Oh, and by the way, I made an appointment to get the lumps checked out."

Tough times can literally mean dark times where we can't see beyond the immediate pain, loss, or confusion. Life feels bleak and we get stuck thinking that it has always been this way and always will be, as if there hasn't been any other time or feeling before. Fear can paralyze us and cause us to think that there is no end to the darkness. At the same time, we yearn for something better. That yearning disconnects us from the present moment and takes us away into the future. We miss the now in the hope that fear will leave. It can become a mental trap as the tightness of the mind extends to tightness of the body.

Yet the darkest moments are the times when we can discover hidden strengths. Both Wendy and I were at a place where we didn't know what to do next. The key is to relax and open into the experience itself. I have stated how essential it is to trust the experience you're having at the moment. Yes, it's hard to do when the experience is so thick with difficult feelings and justified stories, but mindfulness is not about helping you fix an impossible situation. It's about helping you find awareness in a calm, peaceful way so that new strengths can surface to help in your life. There is no magic solution, but there is an awareness path you can follow. With the attitude of mindful curiosity you can discover solutions, reasons, and meaning that might be surprising and unexpected. Try relaxing and getting a little curious about the stuck places in your life. A tense body and mind can't solve anything. It can only keep you stuck, so you might as well notice the tension or darkness and give mindfulness a try.

Exercise: The Dark Moments: Touch and Go

 *20–30 minutes*

This is a challenging exercise that can help you face the dark and seemingly impossible moments. I recommend reading this exercise through first to get familiar with the steps. This exercise will guide you to touch into the challenge, but I don't want you to get overwhelmed by dark feelings. This practice is about "touch and go," which mean you are touching into the difficult feeling enough to be curious and then letting it go so you are not swallowed up by it. Become acquainted with the intensity of your darkness, but don't repeat the pattern of staying in it and getting lost. When you can name what is happening, the intensity may lessen. Allow as much time as you can—at least 20 to 30 minutes—and remember to be patient and kind. Sometimes it works to lean into the intensity, but at other times you may be too triggered or too annoyed to make any progress. Working mindfully with your challenging or dark moments is at the heart of transformation, but they also need gentle care. So if you're not up for it today, then listen to that wisdom and wait. Maybe you can replenish yourself by taking a break and then try it again later. If you can't keep a focus or be mindful, that would be a good time to take a break, reflect, check in with yourself, or see if you need to walk around, sit quietly, or do one of the more body-oriented practices such as "Three-Part Breathing" (under Key 4) or a simple walking meditation (under Key 2) to ground yourself.

1. Set the Right Frame

- Remind yourself that you are training your perception "muscles" to face what is. This is not an exercise for dredging up the pain and getting swallowed by it, so tell yourself you will proceed safely, be kind to yourself, and check in from time to time to see if it feels right to proceed. Remember this is about awareness building and being open to new possibilities or perceptions. Try to be patient with yourself.
- Keep a journal at hand for anything that might be helpful to write down: perhaps an unexpected memory of a person you haven't thought of in a while, or an inspiration for a hobby you forgot you wanted to start. When you hit a challenging spot, ask how this "perceived obstacle" is really a jewel with something to teach you and how you can find the time and

thoughtfulness to discover that aspect. "What is the upside of being laid off my job right now?"

- Set up an image you associate with something neutral or positive: a treasured object, a photograph, a flower. You want it to be something you can gaze at occasionally. This is your resource to come back to.
- Get into a comfortable position sitting up (I don't recommend lying down).

2. Stay and Study

- Allow your attention to be with your body
- Is it heavy, tight, closed? Relax your breath and your body as much as you can.
- Since you are looking at the dark moments, you can call up one of those times in your mind, or you may be in touch with that already. You might be in a heavy mood, or have clenched muscles and become teary-eyed every time you think of a specific situation or crisis. You are "touching in." Get familiar enough to watch, but not so much you are engulfed by the feelings.
- When you feel the familiar gloom or heaviness, gently say to yourself aloud or quietly inside, "Dark moment." You are labeling this darkness in the present moment as it occurs.
- Then look at the image or object in front of you. Notice any positive or neutral qualities. You could name this image or any association you have as you look at it (e.g., "white flower").
- Return to your body again. Notice what is there. Are there the same heavy textures? At times you can tune in to the textural aspect of your body sensations and see what that is like. Take a moment to exhale. This is the "let go" part. You touched in, so now it's time to let go a little. Has the tightness changed? Has the sadness lessened? Does it feel less oppressive? These are the indications that the exercise is working.
- Repeat this process at least five to six times. You are touching in and then letting go, one moment at a time. Alternate your focus between the inner sensations of your body and the image

in front of you. You are shuttling your attention back and forth between these two places (e.g., "dark moment"/"white flower").

- When you feel that there is a shift in the emotional texture or intensity of the darkness, track what that feels like. Let your attention stay with what you perceive as the shift. Keep your awareness on what eases up, such as tension.
- Visit the dark sensations and feelings again. Keep labeling them "dark moment." Touch and go.
- Return to your body awareness and watch how the internal landscape changes. Is there a warmth in your body? An ease in your mood?
- Relax into this completely. Say, *Nothing to fear, just a dark moment.* Touch and go.
- Sit and wait. Realize how the darkness is *just* dark, nothing else. Don't add any story here.
- Continue to track your body with an open and kind attention. Look for places that are at ease or quiet. Notice how you tense up or hold on. Breathe gently into these places that are opening up. Stay with that focus now.
- Stay relaxed-alert in your posture and attitude. If you feel yourself clenching or shutting down, it's okay to stop and let the practice go. If you can continue, keep going, and be with any subtle changes you are noticing.
- Watch for your mind coming in and wanting to narrate the story: *I feel depressed because* . . . In that moment you are stepping into habitual meaning-making. You can notice this, but then let that go too.
- When you feel that there has been a shift, or you are in a different place from where you started, let go of the focus of the exercise, and allow for some reflection.

Remember: If you feel no change or the dark moments get more challenging, or if you are not feeling a sense of relief, please stop. This exercise might be too much for today, or you might

(*continued*)

need to talk about this with a therapist or trusted friend. This is where you need to use your judgment and go further into a place where you can get lost or overwhelmed. This practice is about touching in and letting go as a way to ease the grip of the perceived dark moments. If you feel no immediate relief, seek support. There are times when you may be "too in it." This is okay, and with a caring ear you can get past this. You might consider doing the touch-and-go element of the exercise as you talk to your friend and see if that helps you. That way, you are bringing mindfulness to the way you retell your story and practicing your inner witness while a kind friend listens.

3. Anchor and Harvest

- Write down your thoughts and reflections in your journal afterward.
- Return to a basic mindful awareness and sit with how you feel in your body.

Tools for Recovering From Tough Times

Tough times happen. Having strategies to work with your fears, meet your challenges, and gain insight can turn a seemingly impossible situation into a constructive one. So far, you have been learning about meeting the strong emotions with fearlessness and strength and trusting the process and the experience you are having, even if you are blindly feeling your way through it. You have been weathering and testing your perceptions of your beliefs. I hope at this point you have gained some tools for making it through hard times and developed a new confidence in your body and process.

I am suggesting a pair of exercises to help you further build your set of tools. These can be used every day and not just in a time of crisis. They can help you restore, rejuvenate, and connect back to what you know in your heart to be good and resourceful. The exercise that follows works with the element of Sky and its qualities of openness and reliability. It pairs nicely with the Earth breathing exercise from Key 4. The Sky meditation will remind you of the vastness of the sky, so you can envision a much larger picture of your life. It will help you to cut through the claustrophobia of intensity, fear, and doubt, while the Earth meditation will bring you back to deep and fundamental connections. You can learn to trust, relax, and surrender to a larger wisdom as you remind your body and mind that you and all parts of you, including your spirit, belong to this Earth. No matter how hard life gets, you can come back to this truth. It's simple, really. The sunshine on your face, a fresh breeze at the ocean, the stillness of the trees, and the rustling of leaves in the wind all remind you that you belong.

In both of these exercises, allow nature to become a resource. Even if you live in a city or confined space, you can connect with nature when you notice the sky, feel the air, or see birds flying. You can also recall a time when you were surrounded by trees, on a hill or mountain, or walking at water's edge. Of course, these practices are great to do outdoors, and they can be done together or separate. I recommend repeating them often. The Sky meditation can help you cut through any thickness in your mind. You can rely on it when you are having intense feelings, being pressured or squeezed emotionally, or are feeling claustrophobic. I have my clients do it in my office whenever they feel they are at an impasse. I ask them to look up and find a patch of blue sky. The body and mind respond immediately, because they remember the natural state they want to return to, vast and open like the sky.

The Earth meditation has a grounding effect and is helpful when you feel overly sensitive, at a loss, or shaky. It will stabilize you and bring you back to your body in a grounded way. Let your awareness of the Earth be open. Imagine what it could be like to trust the Earth under your feet. Since the Earth can be warm and spacious, see if you can tap into the safety and warmth of this living, dynamic energy. This practice is about remembering the goodness of your own body, the planet, and your connection with others.

Even if it's tough at first, you can return to feeling well and focusing on what is essential. (As noted, the Earth meditation is under Key 4.)

Exercise: Sky Meditation

 *2–5 minutes*

This exercise can be done for 10 seconds to a minute, anywhere and at any time. It doesn't need a special setup. You just have to remember to notice if something inside you feels too tight, claustrophobic, or stuck. Try this and see what shifts for you.

1. Set the Right Frame

- Set the intention to experiment with your current perspective by opening to the element of Sky. Deliberately interrupt what you are doing, open yourself up to the sky, and see what happens. This can be done anywhere you can glimpse the sky: through your office door, kitchen window, car window, or front door. It is a short practice, designed to interrupt and remind your body and mind that at all times there is a bigger picture.

- Sit or stand facing a window. You can also do this meditation outside in nature. Make sure you can see a piece of the sky. Find even a small patch of open sky if that's all you can see. It doesn't matter if it's cloudy or dark.

2. Stay and Study

- First, have your eyes open, and then gaze downward.
- Let your body settle for a little while.
- See what happens to you when your eyes gaze downward. Are the feelings or thoughts comfortable or familiar?
- Now lift your gaze and look at the sky (not into the sun).
- Let your gaze be drawn into the colors of the sky (blue, gray, etc.) and into its vast open space. If it's nighttime, allow yourself to gaze into the void and observe any light—moon, stars, etc.

- Consider its limitlessness. Dwell on this for a moment.
- Now bring your gaze down. Track the objects in the room or out of doors. How is your view limited by what surrounds you?
- Again, lift your gaze. Find a sliver of the sky. Gaze into the blue, dark, or gray open sky and feel what it's like to open to this much space.
- You are looking at limitless space. Can you rest in this? Are you fearful? What do you think about the limitlessness of space? Does that bring comfort or scare you?
- Let your gaze come down or close your eyes for a moment. This can ground you and bring you back if you feel the sky is too big. The idea is to open your limited view, not get spaced out.
- If you feel spaced out, then come back to a more defined gazing and sense the space around you. Notice the colors and then let yourself return. You don't want to lose yourself, but feel the vastness of space.
- Explore stepping into a bigger picture metaphorically by gazing at the sky for a brief moment. Repeat this several times, for as long as this feels interesting to you and you feel a shift inside. Perhaps any negative or repetitive thinking has stopped, or maybe you don't feel as invested in the problem that's been bothering you.

3. Anchor and Harvest
- Now cast your eyes downward or close them. Has your mood changed? Do you feel more inner space? Do you feel calmer?
- You can test this by thinking about any irritating or intense feelings you began the exercise with. Notice whether these have lessened. Be open to any change you register.

Nothing Lasts

Tough times have the potential to help us weed out the clutter of our lives and see what is essential. Think of the cancer survivor who comes home and wants to rejoice one last time in the loving arms of her family and her rose garden. She remembers the joy she had when she planted the bushes many years ago. Recall Wendy from earlier in the chapter, who deeply feared facing the death of her father and her own immortality. Remember Rick's terror of processing his combat trauma as shown by the numbness of his body. Tough times are not pleasant, but they give us back who we want to be by giving us the opportunity to make a life choice. Will you move on, divorce, give it another try, persist, wait, rethink, fight? These decisions need to come from within you. They need a still place to rest and be heard by you. In the thick of tough times, all you may perceive is never-ending suffering. Call on your resources, strength, and courage to touch into these places of challenge. Remember the Sky and the Earth as physical places you can connect to through your mindful awareness. Find the surprises of your own body and mind when you face your dark places with kindness and acceptance of the present moment. Meet yourself there and find out that nothing lasts—and this is a good thing. This is a centerpiece of the practice of mindfully letting go. You turn toward the source of suffering to discover that your heart is beating, that there is softness at your edges, that you can grieve, let go, cry, or welcome the next chapter of your life. It's possible. Try it. Connect with the Sky, the Earth, your body—right now, right here—and meet whatever stands in your way with ferocity and fearlessness.

Everyday Mindfulness Tip

Use a walking meditation as a resource in your daily life, especially during times of intense busyness or pressure when it may be challenging to take a break. Take small ones, even if you think they are "tiny." These moments of mindfulness add up. Try connecting with the ground underneath you as you walk mindfully around your house. Mindfully step out of your car on your way to the office; pause; look around and take a breath. Even if you have to hurry to the next item on your agenda, take that mini-moment. Notice your body as you climb the stairs or walk to the store or to school. Notice it as you arrive home. Can you feel the exertion in your muscles? Take these short walks in a deliberately slow way. Sense the solidity of the Earth underneath you, feel your breath, and take your steps slowly and mindfully. Work with what you have. Maybe you can't make time for a long meditation right now, but make room for the mini-moments. One of my favorite times for a mindfulness mini-moment is dusk. When the light fades, I suggest you go outside, watch the sun set, and feel into your body the daily rhythm of nature. Do you trust that there will be another dawn? Can you experience this trust in your body?

CULTIVATE INNER CALMNESS

Anything that has a real and lasting value is always a gift from within.

—FRANZ KAFKA

M y client Karen had worked hard to incorporate mindfulness into her life. She took the exercises I taught her, and with regular practice, found ways to slow down, notice her body, and listen to her inner witness. Over time, she reported improved relationships with her peers because she would listen before talking and better absorb what they were saying. She also said she was experiencing moments of spaciousness in the middle of her work day—she would walk more slowly from one end of the office to the other and find opportunities to look out the window and notice her breathing. As a result, she was finding a new sense of confidence and calmness. Previously, she'd had difficulties asserting her viewpoint and would either get angry or withdraw. She had been told she was erratic and disengaged, and as a result she felt unheard. This had created inner turmoil for Karen, and so she became a studious client who practiced her mindfulness daily.

During one session, she described a meeting at work where she was triggered by her supervisor's critical tone. She could feel the pull toward her old habit of expressing anger, but didn't allow herself to do so for fear of retaliation. Instead, she found herself very aware of her body, her breath, and the heat of anger rising inside her. She described this moment as similar to pushing a pause button on her usual reaction. This time, she said to herself, *I am just angry; it's okay. I've got heat in my face and a tightness across my chest.* She could feel a sense of control come back into her posture.

She straightened her spine (she actually remembered my instruction to "be regal!"), then surprised herself by continuing to assert her viewpoint in a calm manner. She later received praise for her clarity.

As Karen recounted this small triumph, she was surprised that she had remained so calm. Even after this tough moment, she still felt afraid that her anger would overtake her. She attributed the fact that it hadn't to her newfound ability to cultivate calmness inside. I agreed. Her practice was taking hold.

If you have worked with the first six keys, you have likely discovered some moments of calmness, rest, and peace in the midst of challenging emotions or circumstances. In this chapter, you will have a chance to deepen this practice and cultivate calmness, coolness, and quietness until they pervade your body and mind and become a steadfast resource. True calmness is a place inside that you can return to for rest. You know what you've been through, you have tools to meet challenges, and you are learning to face life's difficult patches with grace. Now you need to keep practicing to sustain what you've achieved.

Calmness Is a Choice

Cultivating calmness involves making a decision about how you want to approach life. Do you want to live in a more conscious, mindful way, one where you can remind yourself to come back to the present moment and see more clearly what's happening? Or do you choose to live frazzled and out of control, more focused on what happened to you in the past or what will happen to you in the future?

Deciding to live in a more calm, mindful way doesn't mean stressful moments won't happen, but you are now willing to catch them, turn them around, and change how you relate to them. You can be swallowed up by life's challenges, or you can see them, pause, and choose another experience. This decision is entirely up to you. For instance, in the middle of a conversation where you notice you're losing interest or attention, you can say to yourself, *Yikes, I am really bored, I really want to get away from this conversation.* You can befriend the moment by simply stating to yourself what is, focusing on your breathing, and dropping your irritation. Or, when life gets chaotic and confusion swirls around you, you can respond and not react. In the eye of the storm, you can discover that there is something precious inside: a quiet center waiting. You might not be able to see it right away, but the calmness is there, a gift from within, ready to assist when you open your attention.

Thrillers and action films showcase heroes who somehow manage to think clearly in the midst of chaos and save the day. What does it mean in real life to keep a cool head when faced with a crisis? In Western culture, we think of staying cool as being in control and managing a situation. We tend to label coolness as a functioning, thinking, or reasoning strategy. But there is another way to think of this, one that can become a way of being. Other cultures see coolness as having a relaxed and open attitude toward all of life. In this way of thinking, we trust a situation as it is. This doesn't mean being passive or not striving for goals. It means meeting life with a centered calmness so we can make an emotionally grounded, informed decision about how to proceed. In the West African culture of the Itutu, for example, coolness is associated with the element of water and refers to an ever-present mental calmness that is always part of one's actions, approaches, and presence. Being calm is exactly this quality of staying cool within oneself—not heating up or getting reactive, but meeting life's challenges without drama, reactivity, or negativity. Think of people who possess poise as well as an embodied, centered calmness. They have a steady quality about them; they can meet pressure in the same way that they meet pleasure.

So how do you attain this cool way of being and living? Life is not an emergency, and you can move with grace through the tough spots. Coolness is not just a tool for when things get difficult. Moment by moment, you can know your body from the inside out. You can understand what drives your inner fears without having to give in to them. You can learn to discern that an emotional upheaval in the moment is based on a long-standing relational pattern or openly examine thoughts and emotions arising from previous experiences without having to repeat those experiences. You can do this by practicing being present with what is, as it is, again and again. You can find comfort in your own skin and a natural confidence that isn't about showing off but about being okay with who you are.

A Centered Calmness

The Buddha's instructions were simple: Find a quiet place. Sit down and begin to pay attention to your breathing. Simply notice the in and out of your breath and be curious about your experience and sensations. Yet, as you have probably noticed from doing the exercises in previous chapters, sustaining the seemingly simple act of sitting still and inquiring can seem impossible. It is easy to wallow in your sorrows, get distracted, or switch off. When you sit, it helps if you can clarify what you're encountering and understand the terrain. For example, when you notice sleepiness and label it as an obstacle rather than giving in to it, you train your mind to see things as they are. Or you detect a nervous tension and then accept this uncomfortable moment by seeing it for what it is. This insight gives energy and strength to your efforts. Remember that obstacles are disguised jewels, pointing you toward what you may need to wake up about.

Getting to the place where you can be mindful under pressure and be with all of your experiences without reacting takes some practice. This is where finding a baseline of calmness can help. The good news is that your nervous system is set up to remember calmness when given the chance. Every time you return to this natural baseline, your brain strengthens these interconnections. As you learned under Key 4, modern neuroscience calls this the capacity to self-regulate. As infants we need the calming presence of an adult to teach our nervous systems that we are received calmly and lovingly. The loving touch and gaze of a parent communicate this to us.

Many clients have reported to me that when they begin mindfulness practice, it's like they're coming home to a grounded part of themselves that they've forgotten. As if you were coming to rest in the arms of a loved one, you may realize, *This is where I am truly safe and accepted. I feel joyful and peaceful.* Of course, when you didn't have loving arms to receive you as a child, it can make finding calmness more challenging as an adult. You missed out on receiving an early template, but this is where mindfulness has gifts in store for you. Research shows that regular mindfulness practice builds new brain connectivity, which enhances new self-perceptions. This neuroplasticity of the brain results in being able to adapt and change and create positive new experiences that can help reverse harmful thinking and behavior patterns. The obstacle of not knowing how to ground into the body can now become an inspiration to change. You can literally teach your brain and body to get calm, self-soothe, and self-regulate. The new skill of self-regulation directly enhances your ability to soothe anxious thoughts and feelings.

When you first practiced mindfulness, you probably noticed that your mind was often not stable at all. This is called "monkey mind": the endless leaping from one activity, thought, or plan to another. In this state of mind, you are busy and jumpy and never really complete anything because your mind can't slow itself down enough to sustain focus, attention, or discovery. But learning to calm "monkey mind" is another way to practice self-regulation. It's like learning to ride a bike. At first, it takes concentration and focus, and then riding becomes familiar and you begin to trust the process. The neuronal firing that happens each time you have a calming success becomes a memory you can reference. Strengthening this positive brain connection takes repetition. Author and neuropsychologist Rick Hanson (2009) says that our brains are like "Velcro" for negative experiences and "Teflon" for positive ones. This means we need more reinforcement and repetition for the positive experiences to stick and take hold in our brains. The more you "taste" calmness and learn how to cultivate it, the more you realize how good this grounding in the body feels.

Try this:

As you read this chapter, can you sustain your attention? Are you skipping over the page to the end or searching selectively for meaning? Try taking a moment to come back to your breath and then return your focus to the page. See if you can sustain your attention as you read down the page.

Experience Matters

The famous rule that "Neurons that fire together, wire together" (Hebb, 1949) applies directly to training your brain and body for daily mindfulness cues. Strengthening your positive experiences is the key to balancing out your negative ones, for your brain literally needs an average of five "good" experiences to balance out the effect of a single "bad" one [Cacioppo, 1998)]. Survival as a species has dictated that we be vigilant and survive. This makes it more challenging for our calm mental state to dominate. It also means we need to be consistent, train ourselves, and become aware of our tendency to gravitate toward stress and negativity. The next time a beautiful flower or kind gesture catches your attention, see if you can dwell on it; make it a conscious thought and feeling. Say to yourself, *That was a kind moment* or *I really appreciate the color of that apple* or *I cherish the view of the sky*. Add up the cool and fun moments of your life and wire them together as you fire your mindful attention. Leave the survival responses to your body so they can be there to help you out when you need them and not interfere when you are living.

Choosing Calmness During Chaos

Rashmi had had it. She was tired, and now her three-year-old was hurtling a juice box from behind the car seat toward the dashboard. As Rashmi pulled over and got out of the car, she was filled with nervous agitation. Like so many times before when this had happened, she was at her wits' end. She hadn't counted on being a single mom with a child who had neurological issues, and her patience was running thin. She felt attacked, assaulted, and her body was shaking. All the reasoning she was doing wasn't helping much. Of course she loved her child, but in this very moment, it was living hell. Right now, if I had told her to be cool or calm, she might have slapped me!

Have you experienced any moments like these? If you are a parent, these are the times when you may be tired, depleted, exhausted. You want it all to stop and you can see yourself "losing it" or doing something stupid. This is what I call being in the middle of the storm. You have two choices: either to be swept up in it and later regret the emotional outburst, or to recognize this perfect storm and change the channel. Which shall it be? You don't have to be at the mercy of these intense storms; you can actually change this moment by first naming it honestly, to yourself.

Fortunately, Rashmi remembered what we had practiced in my office. She was so angry she wanted to drag her child out of the car and scold him. But she didn't; instead, she recognized her "state," as she called her moment of chaos to herself. Right there, her car parked on the side of the road with the lights blinking, she stood still and noticed her body. She felt herself tremble. She calmed her own inner chaos by finding her tight, fast breath; being present; and then following how her body eventually returned to calmness.

Recall from Key 2 that the way we feel is mirrored by how we breathe (p. 38). A calm body is a smoothly breathing body. A stressed body has erratic breathing patterns to match it. The quickest way to calm is to pay attention and track the kind of breathing you are doing. That sounds counterintuitive, right? When you are in chaos, you tell yourself to calm down and breathe, but I have yet to meet someone for whom that really worked. That's because the body and mind are completely out of sync in that moment. You need to join the body and breath and then teach yourself to regulate downward toward calmness.

Exercise: Calm the Chaotic Moment

 or in the moment in any body position, 2–5 minutes

1. Set the Right Frame

This is an "in-the-moment" mindfulness exercise. You catch it as it's happening. Read the instructions and make an intention to catch these everyday moments. You can practice this exercise by recalling a moment when you were triggered and visualize what you could have done differently.

The idea is to make mindfulness a positive and daily habit in ordinary circumstances. Standing in line at the coffee shop, driving, having a short exchange with someone—these are all opportunities to catch the chaotic moments of your life. They don't have to be big; in fact, pay attention to the small moments of chaos too. Catch a trigger, such as being a little frazzled, or notice how you are sweating and your heart rate is a little faster, or how you just snapped at someone. The first and most crucial step in this meditation is to call or name the moment of chaos. You can speak it aloud, or you can just say quietly, *Okay, here I am. I am in chaos. There it is.*

Make sure you are safe, but don't worry about your current location. Allow yourself to be exactly where you are. You might find yourself in the middle of shopping or some other inconvenient moment. If you find yourself surrounded by other people, you can excuse yourself. Find a quiet place, go outside, go to the restroom or for a short walk. Catch that moment and call that inner chaos what it is. Practice returning to a calm place inside.

2. Stay and Study

Here are the steps to follow after you've recognized the moment of chaos:

- Notice and stay with the chaotic moment you have just called. Really keep your attention on what *it* is. You are naming the feeling, the sensation (*I feel embarrassed* or *I am frazzled and not myself*).
- Track the emotions and sensations that feel as if they are running on high speed. They will pass (remember, everything does!).
- Focus on your breath. Take slower, more deliberate breaths, preferably into your lower belly. Focus on the exhale a little more than the inhale.
- Imagine in the midst of this chaotic moment that you have a calm center. On the outside, the storm is raging, but inside you can come back. Your breath and attention are your helpers.
- Tune in to your body.
- Pay attention to how your body calms. The storm will pass. It will not last.
- Keep following the sensation of calming down. Engage your curious attention.
- Try a gentle smile; lift the corners of your mouth. Bring back some kindness to yourself—perhaps a soft focus or a gentle thought (*I am okay* or *That was intense* or *I am a good person*).
- If there is time to sit down, simply continue to follow your awareness of your breathing.
- The storm has passed and you are okay. How did that happen for you?
- If you find yourself not okay (and that can happen), you may need to connect with someone or take a break. Remove yourself from the situation entirely until you feel more stabilized.

3. Anchor and Harvest

Appreciate and anchor by reflecting on how you turned this moment around. Focus on the positive aspect of what just happened: You have actively changed a potentially negative or damaging moment into a positive one. Where is your awareness now?

Please Note:

There may be times when you can't regulate your breath. If you've had panic attacks before and you think they might return, I suggest bringing your awareness to something on the outside. Focus on your surroundings (another person, the motion of an object, a cloud moving across the sky) and ground yourself by bringing more calm breathing into your belly or the sides of your body (ribs). If this persists or if you have this often, you need to consult a therapist to help you explore the underlying conditions. A panic attack is a bodily response indicating deeper issues that need to be addressed. Being agitated under great stress is normal, but when you place your awareness on your breath, it should eventually regulate and calm. If not, this is an indication that more help is needed.

Tracking and Bearing Witness

He was low to the ground, listening carefully, as if the paw prints had a sound. He lifted his head, and with a broad smile and nod, indicated to his group that the animal was close, really close. This is the beginning of a common ancestral story: the hunter close to the animal he tracks. He listens to the prints on the ground as if they could speak, as if they have a story to tell. He simply follows, observes, listens, and suspends judgment so he can learn and discover.

Tracking your mind and body is a great skill to learn and will help you to cultivate calmness. Initially, you can use tracking with yourself, and later you can begin to use tracking with others. It becomes the vehicle by which you can witness others without judgment. You track and bear witness to what is. In that witnessing, you are suspending any doubt or criticism. You are there, 100 percent. You are alert, calm, and attentive. You are present.

Tracking helped Jennifer stay calm when she witnessed a fatal car accident. She was sitting in traffic when a man suddenly sprinted between cars on a busy Los Angeles boulevard. From Jennifer's perspective, the SUV driver had no chance to stop and collided with the pedestrian, who died instantly. The driver, shocked, stunned, and confused, exited the car. A rush of activity began around him: police, paramedics, the attempt to revive the pedestrian, crying and curious bystanders, the SUV passenger talking on the phone with relatives. No one paid attention to the driver, who stood frozen next to his car, lights blinking in rhythmic fashion. As a bystander on the sidewalk, Jennifer stood witnessing all of this. She saw how the driver's body and mind couldn't comprehend what had just happened, how he was suspended in time. Jennifer knew her ability to help the victim was limited, so she decided to turn her attention to the driver. She slowly walked over to where he stood in shock, put her hand on his shoulder, and calmly told him that she had witnessed the accident. "I saw what happened. He ran right in front of your car. There wasn't anything you could have done. It was so fast. So sudden." The man turned to Jennifer and looked into her kind eyes. Tears began to well up. His face became distorted by grief, and he recounted how he had lost his brother years ago in similar circumstances. Jennifer listened, witnessing his grief and now this tragedy. She softened. That was all she could do: witness, stay calm, and give comfort to a stranger who needed it.

You may have a lot of internal dialogue—judgments, opinions, expectations, emergencies—pushing you around, but you can track what is right there in front of you, become aware, and choose to find the calmness of your being. You may hear yourself say, *Oh, I know this feeling; this is just like when I was in that last bad relationship. I don't like it, and I need to push away what's bad.* But this is closed-door tracking. No newness can emerge; the judgment has been made and the end is already decided! But the experienced, open-door tracker simply looks for information with no bias or judgment of good or bad. It's just data. He or she follows the arc of the journey through varied terrain, which is not judged by the backdrop on which the story unfolds. Moment to moment, the tracker stays awake, following, noticing, encouraged by each new piece of information to continue the journey. When you sit and stay with your experience, you are a tracker on your own unfolding journey. Bold and unafraid, you venture into the internal jungle of your unlived experience.

Tracking is another way of listening to the inner witness that you learned about under Key 2. You are learning to witness your own experiences over and over again, and learning to choose your responses. An overall calmness arrives with this quality of self-witnessing.

Try this:

Try holding off on an immediate reaction. Remember a time when you received distressing news or an instance when you had to make a big decision and didn't take the time you should have to decide. Imagine you could have taken a moment to wait and pause. What would that have changed? Take a mini-moment right now and practice pausing. Lift your gaze, pause, and take a breath. Study your response before you continue reading. Where is your calmness right now?

The Intelligence of Our Awareness

As babies, we learn through our senses. Our touch, smell, taste, and sight are shaped by each experience. We are wired to pay attention to one thing at a time as we determine what helps us survive and what feels good and pleasant. As infants and toddlers, we record nonverbal information, creating a sensory template of what we "feel" our world to be. We are influenced by our culture, family, and religion, and we habituate our experiences to their norms. We learn how to belong and how to fit in. When survival is at stake, our awareness gets switched on as a biological need to self-preserve or be safe. We need to belong, and we will sacrifice our personal desires or intelligence to do so. If we learn that being alive and vibrant is not desired, we begin to conform to this belief and habituate our behavior accordingly.

Sustaining calmness means feeling safe inside yourself and able to be in the world with a sense of belonging and without shame and fear. You are accepting of and connected with who you are. You are home. This is a felt sense, not a thought. But you know when you are home inside yourself and when you are not. The degree to which you find yourself calm and connected is a good measure of this. When you are home within yourself, you are able to have insight and new ideas and engage creatively with the world. You are here right now, and it's good. When a felt sense of calmness and connection comes, you will feel much more aligned with your life. It's an important moment to recognize. You might find yourself in life circumstances that need improvement, but you will have the insight that this moment is right and know you need to be here.

Becoming mindful teaches you "how" you have habituated. You grasp how you have learned to shrink your life—sensations, possibilities, discoveries—in order to conform. Direct experience can show you what you believe in your body and mind. You can safely discover ways to change what you feel is no longer needed.

When you are the tracker of your inner self, experiences arise no matter where you are or what you're doing. Thoughts just come up, one after another. In mindfulness practice, you have a chance to see this phenomenon. Remember that you can choose calmness. You can see what comes up calmly, without needing to attach a storyline to it. You can let it go. The tendency is to grab on to meaning right away. You may want to understand, categorize, compare, dissect, file it and be done . . . and all in matter of seconds. The difficulty is to allow the experience to arise. Just let it come up and say, *Here I am. Hello!* Entertain the possibility that you can just stay with the moment that arises without doing anything else. This is truly one of the hardest things to do, and one of the most valuable ones. Just notice. There is nothing to do but see, feel, and hear what is being displayed. You don't have to change a thing. Choose calmness and return to your breath and your body sensations. Rest in the "being-ness." Let go of any story or thoughts.

In the process, you may discover that there are a lot of thoughts that are repetitive, or you may find yourself searching for answers. Watch your inner entertainer and the obsessive recycler of old stories. Then let it go. Unglue yourself from the repetitive nature of your thinking processes. Trust in the mindful space without the thoughts. See if you can practice noticing what your mind throws up and then let it go.

I recommend here that you return to an earlier exercise in this chapter ("Calm the Chaotic Moment"). Train your awareness; it needs practice. Choose the calmness over the recycled stories in your head. Follow up with a short journaling session if you wish to record the obstacles you encounter. Which are your favorites? It helps to write them out so you can see what they are and how they sound. Now turn to an exercise similar to one you've done before, but this time with a focus on letting your experiences arise and returning to a calm state of being.

Exercise: Returning to Calmness

 *20–30 minutes*

This practice can help you shift your bias toward a state of calm. You want to practice choosing a positive, calm experience. In addition to becoming aware of what is present, you can make a deliberate choice to return to a positive association, such as an image of your favorite place or a person you admire who possesses the qualities of calmness and coolness that you seek. In this exercise, you are interrupting the habit of putting up obstacles in your own way. Remember, the more familiarity you build with positive experiences, the more you counterbalance the negative ones.

1. Set the Right Frame
- Sit and settle your body into your familiar relaxed-alert mindfulness posture. Set an intention to find calmness.

- Witness what is present for you right now. Track your breath and whatever else is in your attention.
- Call up a familiar place that you associate with calmness, perhaps a sensation or image you associate with being calm. A person who embodies the calmness you admire is helpful here too. Visualize the person or capture the feeling of his or her presence with you in this moment. What happens as you call up his or her presence?
- Allow your breath to settle.

2. Stay and Study
- Track anything unsettling (e.g., thoughts, a compulsion to return to the issue at hand, any bodily discomfort).
- Become outwardly very still. Wait.
- Track whatever thoughts, images, or ideas arise, one at a time (if you can), and label them ("thought arising," "image arising," "idea arising," etc.).
- Return to your calm place (your imagined or sensory one) with a focus on returning to your purpose. You are now making a choice to return to the positive place.
- Repeat that focus toward the positive image or person, feeling it or him or her as many times as you like.
- Pay attention when you get distracted or want to make up a story.
- Observe all the players, the scenery, the details of your positive resource, as if you are filling a canvas with multiple colors. You might be pulled right into the storyline again, but let that happen.
- Then return to the calm resource again.
- You are aiming to shuttle your attention back and forth until you can feel a more stable attention resting on the positive image or association.
- See if you can detect a quality of "resting in the calm." This might be a longer time without distracting thoughts, or a sense of peace, or a "nothingness" where you are just calm and present.

- Now drop the whole thing.
- Return to your body, breath, and the present moment and see what *kind* of calmness is here now.
- Check it out. See if there is something new that you haven't paid attention to previously. Perhaps there is a sense of sweetness, a tear, some sadness? Maybe some open space or nothingness? Can you trust this new calm? Does it resemble the person you admire?

3. Anchor and Harvest

- Try sitting for a while with utter openness.
- Write down your experience and reflect on what it takes to bring these calm qualities into your life on a more regular basis. What needs to happen in your routines of daily living to make room for mindfulness? What are some small steps you can initiate to remind yourself to calm and center yourself? What has worked so far? What can you build on? Is there an exercise in this book that has been particularly helpful?

A Note About Stress: Easing the Effects With Calmness

Stress is a normal occurrence. Prolonged stress is not. Trauma and overwhelming stress are taxing for our bodies and minds and need to be helped in a professional manner. Mindfulness can help with these, but I advise you to consider the guidance of an experienced meditator or health practitioner if you find yourself experiencing trauma (see the Resources section at the end of the book). You are built to handle a fair amount of stress, given that it will be followed by periods of rest, but over the long term, stress affects the body. Symptoms range from irritability, sadness, depression, and lack of interest to fatigue and a host of somatic complaints. Clients come to me with inexplicable headaches, digestive issues, body tension that is not easily released, extreme fatigue, and long-lasting symptoms that affect the body and mental state. The secondary effects of stress include unhealthy habits such as poor diet, little sleep, lack of exercise, self-medication with alcohol and smoking, and other addictive behaviors. Unfortunately, 75 percent of the general population will experience overwhelming stress at some point in their lives, so we all have to learn how to be with stress, whether it affects us directly or those in our lives. According to one statistic, 54 percent of Americans are worried about their stress levels. Mindfulness is a great way to learn how to cope and heal from its damaging effects.

Stress is the great interrupter of our life force. We get derailed into survival responses and our creative expression shrinks. Stress teaches our attention to be either locked in and super-focused or frazzled and disjointed. The effects are grave: We become inattentive, clumsy, scattered, and ultimately nonproductive in our lives and work. When stress is culturally endorsed by our society, we learn to just live with it. Why? The threshold has dramatically shifted over the last decade. The number of stress-related illnesses has climbed, and we take for granted that this is how it is. Stress also disrupts our natural state of calmness. We can barely remember that calmness is our baseline, that this is who we are. We assume stress, speed, and agitation are the new normal, yet they are a sure path to dis-ease. We need to recognize that being calm is who we need to be and that we can cultivate calmness even when stress is high and all-pervasive.

The body holds on tightly to its stress responses for a reason. When you smother feelings you don't want to feel, anxiety or fear might arise. Over time, this chronic denial of feelings becomes a bottled-up inner tantrum. The adult version resembles that of a two-year-old going "Waaaaaa . . . that is so unfair! I don't like it!" These cumulative, mini-moments of anxiety get stored in the body, and at the end of the day you are tense, upset, and tired or exhausted just from getting through the day. As you get in touch with these layers and unwind, you might find that your sadness and anger are engulfed by the drama of daily events. What would it be like if you let them be? Can you allow for the irritations of the day to be present? Imagine the textures of daily irritations and tensions riding through you like a moving set of clouds. You can be present with them and at the same time not indulge the feelings. Witness what is happening and reenact the drama of it, and then you can begin to see that you are a calm and spacious being to begin with. Spend less time whipping up the frenzied dramas of the day and pay more attention to how these feelings show up. Return to Key 6 exercises and repeat these, as well as the chaos-calming exercise from earlier in this chapter. Remember that calmness, not stress, is your basic mental state. Take care of yourself by recognizing that it's not okay to be stressed. Make time for yourself to return and cultivate the calmness in yourself. It is there. It might take a while to get back, but it's there.

Calming Will Put Me to Sleep

It's common in mindfulness meditation to come up against the hurdle of being tired. The body relaxes, the mind lets go, and the cues of tiredness come forward. It is not unusual to fall asleep during meditation exercises. Don't feel badly about this. Can you make some room for this awareness of being tired to be important? Your body is communicating directly to you that you need to rest. Most of us don't pay enough attention to the cues of our bodies and override the tired signals. Long working hours, endless to-do lists, and busy lives take a toll. Our natural circadian rhythm follows a twenty-four-hour cycle of light and darkness and triggers hormone releases that indicate tired and awake phases. See if you can become more in tune with these natural rhythms. What would it be like to listen more carefully to how your body functions best and when it needs rest? How you have spent your energies during the day becomes very apparent when you get quiet and sit down on the meditation cushion. Part of establishing a mindfulness routine involves noticing when is the best time for you to practice. If you practice at night, for instance, you might notice that you fall asleep easily, and so you might use the exercises in the book to help you rest instead. During the morning, you might be more refreshed and use the exercises to energize yourself and set your intentions for the day. During the day, you might find a few moments to practice the exercises and stabilize your energy or cue your mind to slow down and connect with your body. See what works for you and experiment with different times. If you fall asleep, don't fret about it; allow for some much-needed rest and try again later.

Try this:

Next time you yawn, pay attention to how tired you are. What are some of the signs of your fatigue? What happens in your body as you yawn? Can you let the tiredness be there, or are you pushing through the fatigue? What choice can you make right here? Grab a coffee? Try pausing instead and pay attention to how the tiredness in the body actually feels. Take your tired body on a short, slow walk.

Quiet Versus Stillness

As a remedy for her prolonged stress after a financial hardship, Amy decided she wanted to get away and have some time for herself. A generous friend offered her a small vacation cabin in the woods. Amy settled in and looked forward to enjoying her retreat— away from her partner and her beloved animals, far from her daily chores and the recent money stress. She had always loved the redwoods. They reminded her of trips she had taken with her family when she was a little. The tall trees were majestic and calm. She stood outside on the deck, then settled into her reading chair. It was quiet, but inside her head, all she could hear was the recent argument she'd had with her partner. She recalled details of the conversations they'd had about their differences in handling a botched investment they had recently made together. She felt angry and betrayed by her partner's lack of follow-through. She spent her precious time at the cabin stewing over the details of the dialogue, but then recognized how disconnected she was from the quiet woods she loved so much. It all looked different to her, bleak and somehow not as nice as she had remembered it. She regretted coming.

In the quiet, we can hear the inner noise loud and clear. The internal noises get amplified, and this can be difficult to bear. After a while, Amy could hardly be present in the quiet woods. All she could hear were the internal dialogues of her conflicts. In her mind, she turned over the details of the financial distress she was facing and anticipated the pending foreclosure of her house. Her stress level was continuing.

The journey to calmness and stillness can be a messy one. You may be confronted with what's been activated in your life, what you want to escape from, or how agitated you are. That's the whole point. You get in touch. But when you can stay with that noise and see through it, the quiet will develop into stillness and the smallest occurrence can become delightful. Find a quiet place, a park, a quiet corner of the house, anywhere where you can get away for a moment and listen to the surrounding sounds of birds, water, traffic, wind. Let any stillness you can find arise. Soon you may feel in sync. You can arrive and simply be with yourself. Striving and battling fall away. Stillness becomes a friend.

Of course, Amy could not go there at first. The quiet surroundings exacerbated the loudness of her emotions. The quiet became an irritant. She had to sit through the battle of her inner turmoil. But sit she did, staying and listening to both the inner noises and outer quiet. She went on walks occasionally, sitting down here and there to follow her breath and tune in to what was present for her in that moment. As she repeated this mindful walking, an inner stillness finally arrived. At first she noticed an absence of the inner dialogue that had incessantly been going over the details of her anguish. The turmoil of her last months began to recede into the background. She became aware of the rock she sat on, the smell of the woods, how the moss felt to her touch. The stillness of the forest was intermittently pierced by woodpeckers drilling into dead trees, the sounds of singing birds, and the gentle squeaking of branches in the breeze. As she became aware of the surroundings, she noticed her inner quiet coming to the foreground. Sadness and confusion arose, and she felt kindness arise toward her own feelings of being overwhelmed. Her disappointments were allowed to be, and with that the stillness deepened. She got a real break from her daily life and saw how stressed she had been living inside herself.

There is a difference between getting quiet and tuning in and discovering true stillness. Stillness arrives after you have become quiet. Stillness is dynamic and alive; it is not at all a dead space. "Nothing is happening; it's so boring," I've heard students lament when they try to get in touch with stillness—but that is not stillness. Their complaints of boredom mean their minds are searching for meaning or for entertainment. We are used to consuming and expecting to be entertained most of the time. Left to experience stillness, most of us are not trained to know what to do.

Cultivating true inner calmness takes time and patience. You need stretches of time where your body can get quiet and your mind is free from distractions so you can discover the calmness underneath. This next exercise takes some time, so make it your intention to give that to yourself. If you do so after practicing earlier exercises in the book, you will realize great rewards, for the other exercises have prepared you to do a longer sitting. You now have the know-how to track and witness your mind and body and bring your breath and body with you. Go ahead and make time for a longer sitting. The more often you repeat this, the more you will become familiar with your body and mind patterns. They will become intimate friends, and what you know, you can let go of more easily.

Exercise: Observing the Space of Silence

 *30–45 minutes*

This exercise is about creating a personal retreat. Select a time or day during the week where you can spend a prolonged time in silence. Make the intention to take that time to practice, for it doesn't work well to squeeze this exercise in between activities such as appointments. Allow spacious timing before and after your practice. You might start by doing the exercise for 30 minutes at a stretch; you can increase the length of time as you repeat the exercise. The goal is to make a conscious effort to be silent. After the formal sitting period, try to continue to observe the silence as you do your everyday tasks, such as cleaning up around the house. Slow down your ordinary activities and see what that feels like. The ideal would be to take this time in nature, either sitting or walking, but all in silence.

1. Set the Right Frame
Here is a structure to play with:

- Spend the initial 5 to 10 minutes simply sitting or lying down and resting your body.
- Allow your mind to settle. Use the labeling technique (e.g., "thinking" or " I am letting it go").
- Track your breath and connect with your body, taking inventory of where you are at today.

2. Stay and Study
- Sit up and spend the next 30 minutes in silence. Check your sitting-up posture and remind yourself to have your hips aligned underneath your shoulder girdle, you neck in alignment with your shoulders and hips. Make sure there is no or little tension in your body by sitting comfortably.
- When your body is quiet and settled, focus on your breath and the inner landscape of your feelings and sensations. Let the quiet internal space expand by focusing on your breath and not entertaining any stories.
- See if you can connect with your calm self here.
- Allow yourself to come back to your breath and your body if you get distracted.
- Journey through the layers of your awareness until you can enjoy the silence.

- Thoughts will come and go. Watch them and let them go.
- Be present with yourself and your breath awareness.
- Track when you feel calm and see if you can be present even more.
- If it gets too tough and you can't continue, remember that these are just obstacles (jewels) on your journey. Note what they are. Let them be. Breathe and hang in there; it will pass. Try again. That is what practice is about.
- If you truly feel you can't stay with being still and quiet, then take a break. Make sure you don't entertain yourself but rather take a mindful break. Enjoy a view out the window, fix a snack with awareness, or take a short walk.
- Come back to your formal sitting again. Observe whether it feels different now.

3. Anchor and Harvest
- Spend 15 to 20 minutes journaling. Continue to write from this silent space if you wish.
- It may also be helpful to go for walk in nature and notice how your world looks to you now. Observe your thoughts and insights. After a longer sitting practice, you may be able to watch your thoughts more clearly and distinguish between genuine new insights and habitual rumination.

Extending the Space of Silence: Suggestions for a Longer Mini-Retreat

Over time, you can increase the length of this exercise to half a day and then a full day of silence. Perhaps create a regular mini-retreat for yourself. You can design a personal mental health day for yourself by clearing your schedule and taking a day off to devote to mindfulness practice. Spend a day in silence not interacting with your email, phone calls, or the demands of your life. It's essential to create a clear structure ahead of time and make sure you don't get distracted. Initially, it's not so easy to sit half a day or a full day in meditation. You may want to break it up by doing walking meditations. I recommend sitting for at least 30 minutes; you can then break up the sitting with a 15-minute walking meditation or a short bathroom or snack break, and then return to another period of sitting. One of the sitting periods can involve somatic practice, such as three-part breathing or Earth breathing (see Key 4). Adapt the structure of this exercise according to your needs. At the end, make sure you leave time to write and reflect. That way you can not only record what happened but also see deeper meanings in your practice time.

What arises in the meditations as insight and new thoughts is often very interesting to think about. In the meditation, you don't want to dwell too long on this, as your focus is on clearing and being with what comes up and not on developing a new storyline or plan. But in your writing and reflection, you can take some time to pick up the interesting insights you had or the new plans you came up with and develop them. This is where mindfulness practice begins to support your life in a concrete and sustaining way. You begin to develop an inner dialogue and reflect on what is important in your life. You may also benefit from looking over the writing exercises in this book (pp. 128, 133, 142, 146, 169, 188). Use them to get you jumpstarted.

Make the Effort

There is a big difference between being mindful in your daily life and formally practicing mindfulness by sitting and walking for a specified period where being mindful takes center stage. Clients often tell me that they play golf, hang out with their cat, or take hikes, and that this is their mindfulness time. That is a great start! I call these mini-mindfulness moments, but they are not the same as setting aside time to sharpen your mindfulness as a tool. Think of your gym time. When you go for an occasional hike, it's a lovely activity, but it's not the same as doing regular workout sessions at the gym where you deliberately strengthen certain muscle groups or work your cardiovascular system. The repetition of those crunches or those intervals on the treadmill yield results because you are doing them again and again. Your mind is no different. You need repetition of your mental activity to train for a stable mind. The test comes when you sit down to practice and you see how challenging it is to not think and be spacious. It actually takes effort, some time, and a clear choice to make taking care of your mind a priority.

Cultivate calmness in your life with both short and long periods of practice and retreat. It's worth it. I strongly believe that in our busy times, taking care of your mental state and learning how to listen to your body is a necessity, not a luxury. You need stillness to hear what truly moves you, to let go of what you no longer need, and to make decisions with clarity of mind. You need stillness so you can find yourself again and feel good about who you are. Treat your mental state like a precious gem that needs loving care to sparkle. Take a moment and reflect on how you can bring a regular mindfulness practice into your daily routine and commit to a daily meditation. Take one realistic step toward incorporating what you are learning here into your life.

Everyday Mindfulness Tip

Since you are working in this chapter to apply mindfulness to all areas of your life and create new mindful habits, reflect on where you are not being mindful in your life. Are there routines that you do every day that you could add mindfulness too? When you work out at the gym, can you change it up and not use the TV monitor or iPod to work out to and instead listen to your body? What about cooking breakfast or dinner? Putting away the dishes, doing laundry, or brushing your teeth? How about your time with your partner? You can apply mindfulness to your conversations by taking more time to listen rather than immediately responding. Can you bring mindfulness into your sex life? Pay attention to your routines: What do you do every single day that you are so accustomed to you don't even think about it anymore? Examine your habits and ask yourself where you can add some mindfulness. You might be chopping vegetables, feeding your pet, or watering the plants. These seemingly ordinary moments are perfect occasions to pay attention to your breath, notice your body movements, and allow the mundane to become interesting because you are slowing down to watch. These moments work best with activities that you can do silently or by yourself, such as ordinary household chores. Of course, you can extend mindful awareness to how you use your media. Pause before you fire off that angry text. Put the phone down when you receive a text, a message, or a tweet that triggers you. Give it some space, then respond.

CHOOSE ABUNDANCE

Abundance is the quality of life you live and quality of life you give to others.
—J. K. ROWLING

The previous chapters invited you to learn how to ride your physical sensations and emotions and accept them as they are: bright, challenging, and intelligent. If you have worked through the exercises, you have found that awareness of your breath and body is a resource and anchor. Through the storms, you may have discovered calm moments and how to rest in them.

Initially, the benefits of practicing mindfulness may include decreased levels of stress, an improved sense of well-being, and a more balanced approach to life. Once you see that this is doable, your appetite for more may arrive, and you may strive to increase these feelings. Remember my client Rick, the veteran from Keys 3 and 4? He was inspired by his own healing to help others. He wanted to share the tools he had learned to ease his body and mind. He decided to go to school to be trained as a counselor. Eventually he began to teach mindfulness classes to fellow veterans and share his insights. Rick's story of healing was inspiring to others, and this in turn enriched his life and increased his own sense of well-being. Kindness, compassion, gratitude, abundance—they all build on each other in this way.

Living more abundantly is a choice, not an accident of fortune or luck. This can take the form of committing to a regular mindfulness practice and consciously bringing an increased sense of awareness to how you interact with family and friends and community. Or you may choose to express gratitude on a daily basis or find a concrete way to help others. All that is required to live abundantly are small acts of conscientious change. No step is too small. Remember that slowing down and being with your experience and learning to accept what is *is* the work of abundance. Denying your experience or your feelings, whether they be laughter, tears, or anger, is the opposite.

Scarcity Thinking

The state of scarcity is the opposite of an abundance state of mind. When you think, *I'm not good enough, I can't do . . . , I will never be as . . .* , or *Why don't I have . . . ?*, you are engaging in scarcity thinking, meaning you are looking for the deficits in your being. In these moments, you are not looking at what is good, whole and abundant; rather, you are comparing yourself to others or ruminating on what you don't have or how a hurtful incident from long ago makes you feel victimized. Scarcity thinking is rooted in fear and negative experiences you have not fully come to terms with or integrated. For example, the fear of not being accepted in a community might cause you not to assert your viewpoint. Anxiety about not having enough might make you hesitate to reach out to someone in need. The fear of not being good enough might dampen any desire to take risks. You can think of all these hurdles as obstacles, and as you have learned from the 8 Keys, the obstacles are really jewels in disguise. You can choose to buy into your fear and be ruled by it, or you can make a conscious effort to look for new perspectives. There are many reasons why you may see through the looking glass of "not enough"—most of them are fear-based, but some may also be rooted in a helpless sense of not knowing how to address your fears.

Cliff lived his life focused on scarcity. Even though he had a well-paying job, friends who stuck by him, fine health, and a son who adored him, his mind would continually return to how he felt betrayed by his ex-wife. The divorce had happened five years before, yet he was unable to let go and move on. Each time he talked about his loss, he lived in the emotional ruin of his life. His scarcity thinking had become an addiction, a strange and familiar discomfort that he returned to again and again. He was afraid to move on because he would have to acknowledge that the breakup was permanent. Living in emotional limbo provided a familiar feeling that he was still in a relationship with his ex-wife, and the deep grief of this loss was also a connection to the past. He was afraid to be happy and let go. He was so invested in what was not good about his life that he missed what was lovely and positive. He couldn't relinquish the pain and the disappointment he had experienced. At the urging of a friend who had had enough of listening to his stories, he signed up for a six-week class in mindfulness meditation and discovered how discursive and ruminating his mind was. Cliff was shocked to see how he was repeating the same stories of betrayal and having the same bad feelings again and again. Luckily, practicing meditation helped him to see this pattern more clearly. Initially, he got in touch with the fear of becoming a divorced, single dad, but more importantly he began to see his whole life. He realized that he had not paid much attention to the benefits of having a stable community and a solid, loving relationship with his son. As he included this awareness in his mindfulness practice and began to soften toward the pain of the past, he began to discover the abundance inside and let go of what was no longer useful.

Try this:

Pause for a moment and reflect on your scarcity thinking. As you read Cliff's story, can you resonate with the fear to move on? Are you afraid at times to fully embrace what is good in your life? What happens in your body as you touch into this theme? Any tightness or discomfort? Try breathing and softening into any tension, or let it be. Maybe it has something to tell you.

Abundance as a Perspective

Many of my clients and students complain that their lives are lacking an overall sense of meaning. They might feel okay in a vague, undefined sense, but as one client said, "I can't find true satisfaction anymore; everything seems all right, but not fulfilling. I am not happy." Often clients feel they can't have enough, be enough, or get enough, or else when they do get enough of something, the sense of satisfaction leaves. You can think of this feeling as a kind of scarcity thinking. Just like Cliff, you may not be looking at what is actually going well or feels good. Remember from Key 7 that your brain is "Velcro" for negative experiences and "Teflon" for good ones? (Hanson, 2009). Paying attention to these tendencies is the key to transforming scarcity thinking. Reggie Ray, a meditation teacher, has said that we need to first touch inner stillness before we can perceive the abundance that is there (Ray, 2008b). When you feel your body again, you return to feeling and sensing who you really are. You can appreciate and laugh at yourself.

What does it mean to you to feel a sense of abundance? Is it having everything you need and want? Does it mean fulfilling all your hopes and dreams? Does it mean never having to worry about anything again? Or does it simply mean that you are alive and breathing? Consider this possibility: What if you can allow something that may seem small to feel big, fulfilling, good, meaningful? What if abundance is already present in your life at this moment?

Many years ago, when studying in Java, Indonesia, I went for my morning stroll through the local market. It was a lively place brimming with merchants, buyers, food, spices, and fabrics. I paused at the stand of an old woman selling *batik*, the traditional brightly colored cloth. After an intense and playful negotiation, we settled on a price. She took the fabric and began wrapping it with an equally colorful paper. I wasn't in a big hurry, but it seemed as if she took forever to wrap it. I could barely stand to watch. Her wrinkled hands glided over every fold, straightening the tiniest

crease before wrapping the paper. Each of her strokes was per-
formed with careful, tender attention. I was drawn into this almost
ceremonial moment. I noticed how out of place my impatience
seemed. Her finishing touch was a complicated bow that held the
package in place. I was utterly entranced. Her gliding and wrapping movements were so practiced—I was sure she had done this a
thousand times. What made this memorable wasn't her artful
wrapping but her complete attention to the task, and her obvious
enjoyment of it. Her proud achievement was complete when she
handed me the package with a grin.

If abundance has everything to do with perspective, you might,
for example, look at a branch and think of it as a brown twig, or
you can look more closely at the same branch and see how it is the
furthermost extension of the tree's root system and an intricate life-
form brimming with energy. In the market, I could have opted
to focus on the overwhelming scents and the colorful activities
around me, or I could have gotten stuck in my impatience. All of
those were there, and I was aware of them, but in that one moment,
I slowed myself down and chose to be present with the woman
who was selling me the cloth. In the same way, as you observe the
tree branch, you may consider it to be plain or even insignificant,
but you can also observe the tree's green and lush foliage bursting
forth, hosting small bugs and insects. As you look at this tree, how
do you think of it in this moment? Abundant or lacking? Can you
see yourself from this viewpoint? Just like that tree, you are alive
and splendid, perfect in your complexities, liveliness, and imper-
fections. What would it be like to view yourself as abundantly alive
even if you have challenges at this time in your life? Choosing
abundance is not frivolous or superficial, but a courageous choice
about how to live, and that also means recognizing the times when
you don't feel in touch with the abundance in your life. Whenever
you feel well and content, make the choice to recognize this as
abundance in the moment. And then give yourself credit for being
brave or strong enough to do so.

When you experience scarcity, pain, or suffering, it can be
helpful to look at how you are with these feelings. You may carry

unknown expectations and views that you "should be happy" or that you "deserve better than this." Of course, there are many kinds of suffering, and loss, pain, and traumas are subjective experiences. There are events in your life that just happen. You do not wish them on yourself or others. The question becomes not how to prevent pain but how to engage with it. How you view and deal with your pain is an essential focus. How do you choose to meet it? Are you curious and open?

A Taoist story from ancient China about a poor farmer illustrates one way of reframing expectations about luck and misfortune. A farmer and his son had only a few possessions, the most important of which were their prized animals. One day, one of their horses ran away. "What bad luck," the neighbor lamented.

"Who knows," the farmer replied. A few weeks later, the horse returned, bringing with him four more horses.

"What good luck," the neighbor called out.

"Who knows," the farmer replied. The next day the son attempted to ride one of the new horses, fell off, and broke his leg.

"What bad luck," the neighbor lamented again.

"Who knows," the farmer replied. The following week the army drafted all the young men in the area, sparing the farmer's son, who was in bed with his broken leg.

"What good luck," the neighbor said.

"Who knows." the farmer replied.

If we take a scarcity perspective, we may conclude that the farmer is indifferent, uncaring, or depressed. If we consider this story from an abundance perspective, we could also say the farmer allows for a wide range of possibilities and outcomes. He waits and trusts. He does not assess that life is treating him well or poorly. He does not live in a state of expectation or feel that he deserves more than he's been given. He trusts the process as it unfolds, and stays present in the moment, for he doesn't know what may happen in the future.

In a similar way, you can reframe your own life from an abundance perspective and be open to the possibilities. Go ahead. Who knows!

Exercise: Reframe the Inner Critic

 15 minutes

Choosing abundance doesn't mean you aren't acknowledging wrongdoing or pain. It also doesn't mean you're pretending everything is good when it's not. This exercise takes a look at how your inner critic may be reigning inside of you, reminding you to focus on the wrongdoing or pain. Take your time writing and discover what the particular messages are here for you. Know that your experience is intelligent even if you can't discern it yet. Reframing is about adopting a fresh, new perspective and looking for abundance opportunities.

1. Set the Right Frame
- Sit for a moment, positioning yourself in your familiar physical posture.
- Take a few conscious breaths and settle the busyness of your mind.
- See what is there without following any thought.
- Check into your body and see what is there right now.
- Make the intention to write with a mindful and kind inner posture.

2. Stay and Study
- Take a piece of paper, and divide it into two columns.
- In one column, write down any internal, critical voices you can recall or that are operating right now. Line by line, write down the critical statement (e.g., "I am not achieving enough").
- When you're finished, take a moment and settle into mindfulness. Remember your goodness and the abundance attitude.
- In the other column, next to the criticism, write down the reframing thought (e.g., "I know how to take my time" for "I am not fast enough").
- Contemplate the value underneath the negative statement; that is, what is the statement under the statement? Could

"You are not good enough" reflect something about how you conduct yourself? Maybe you don't really want to be fast, as that is not your natural pace.

- Take each line and reframe the negative statement by finding its intelligence or possibilities.

3. Anchor and Harvest

- Let go of the writing and just sit quietly.
- Let your mind and body settle.
- See what arises naturally. Pay attention to any new thoughts or feelings.

Softening Into Kindness

Abundance is the physical and emotional sense of well-being that comes from feeling nourished and at peace. Being kind to yourself is one way to cultivate abundance, but how do we get there? One way is to practice being "soft" by using your exhalations to cue a softer awareness. In many of the exercises in this book I have asked you to pay attention to your exhale as a way to release tension in your body. Softening your out-breath, releasing tension, and paying attention to your body with gentleness are all ways to soften.

Try this:

In my meditation classes, I often tell my students to soften their gaze. Read these instructions first and then attempt the following: Take your eyes off the page, bringing your gaze downward without focusing on anything. Soften your gaze by releasing your eye muscles. Let your breath be soft and long. What happens with your attention? Any softness here? What would it be like if you could hold this soft approach? As you move through your day, relax your laserlike gaze toward others and take each person in with soft eyes. What happens when you do?

What makes you feel content and abundant will be different than it is for someone else. Yet the process of discovering what it takes to live more abundantly may require some reflection and a deeper understanding of your habits. Suffering can dominate your experience so that you can't see the abundance in front of you. Remember that it's easier to look for what is not there than to appreciate what is. Start looking (softly!) for what is there. Play with making a conscious effort to find abundance and adopt this as a point of view. Remind yourself to look at a current dilemma or troubling situation from an abundance perspective.

Extend Abundance: Stop and Feel Gratitude

Grace was on her way to an appointment. Unfamiliar with the area of town, she had arrived 40 minutes too early, but the street didn't offer much in the way of restaurants or coffee shops and it was pouring rain. As Grace walked along the street looking for cover, she saw a church with its door ajar. After a moment of hesitation, she opened the door, and a warm and brightly lit chapel greeted her. Grace decided that this was a good place to wait out the rain and took a seat in a wooden pew. She closed her eyes, slowed down from her hectic day, and settled in. She sensed a worn but firm wooden seat beneath her.

A wave of tears amid a feeling of gratefulness for this little sanctuary suddenly rushed forth. Grace became aware that all over the world, many people are in need of a protected place to be quiet. She felt a profound connection with those in mosques, temples, and churches, who were at this very moment sitting quietly and feeling sheltered. It didn't matter what religion or country they or she belonged to: All were welcome. Grace imagined people long before her with a vision to create places of peace for others to come and pray, rest, reflect, and worship in the way they believed. She was surprised by this strong and sudden gratefulness. She was touched by the power of what it meant to go inside herself, yet feel in connection with others. She opened her eyes and looked around.

Sprinkled throughout the pews were men and women in deep contemplation. Suddenly, Grace wished them well. She was filled with her own abundance in this moment and naturally wanted to extend this to others. Grace could have been annoyed at being rained on and having to wait for her appointment, but she chose to explore and expand the possibilities by tapping into her own feelings of gratitude.

You might be familiar with the idea of looking at life as a glass half empty or half full. Getting stuck in old perceptions has everything to do with how you perceive the world around you. In your everyday life, you can look for confirmation of your beliefs as they are and not look for an alternative. Just as Grace's moment in the church and the story of the poor farmer illustrate, maybe an unfortunate or irritating situation will turn out to be a blessing, or maybe it's okay just as it is. Practice suspending judgment and wait to see what is. What if the person you are talking to has something unexpected to offer? At times I interrupt my teenager as he rolls his eyes to see if he can pause and listen first before responding. His developing teenage brain sometimes causes him to be reactive and less patient. At those times, I gently remind him to pause and wait. This brings a mindful moment to a habit such as interrupting others.

If you want to cultivate an abundance perspective, then begin to look for small opportunities to practice. Consider pausing to see if you can feel gratitude as you interact with others. Notice that you can extend your abundance by stopping and paying attention to the world around you.

Try this:

Practice everyday abundance by pausing during the day and looking around your workplace, your home, your garage, the store. Try stopping to feel gratitude when you are in the carpool lane picking up your kids, or when you are in transit on the train.

(continued)

Find something that feels good about this right now. At the end
of your day, pause once more and reflect: *What was new or positive today? Did someone smile at me? Did my partner or child give
me a hug or kiss? Did I enjoy the rain, clouds, or sun? What can I
be grateful for?* Take a breath; feel your heart. What does your
heart have to say about this day? Give yourself a full minute and
soak in whatever goodness or gratitude you experienced. Think,
feel, or sense all of its qualities, textures, and details.

The Biology of Kindness

At first, the idea of spending a cold evening outdoors and serving
strangers didn't appeal to Trevor. "I don't know these people," he
said in the weeks leading up to a campus-sponsored event, where
students were asked to serve food at a local outdoor food kitchen
for the homeless. Trevor and his friends were part of a service-
learning group that provided young adults with opportunities to
serve their local community. Rationally, Trevor understood that
helping others was a good activity. He liked the idea of helping, but
he was nervous.

Putting on oversized surgical gloves to ready himself to serve
the food, Trevor had a calm look on his face. He decided to focus
wholeheartedly on the task at hand. Person after person walked up,
and he took the time to quietly make eye contact before asking
them their food preferences. "Good evening, sir," he said, "Would
you like shepherd's pie or lasagna?" There was a pause each time
as the recipient considered his or her choices. Carefully, Trevor
spooned the food onto the plate, then gently offered it to the person in front of him. A shy smile flitted across his face when the
recipient met his eye gaze. Again and again, the person thanked
him or nodded his or her head in a respectful gesture. A quiet and
ancient ritual of exchange, sharing, and caring through food
brought out a feeling of bodily kindness in both server and receiver.
A hundred people later, Trevor was still offering each person the

same quality of care, with a sense of freshness each time. He did not tire. In this minimal, almost silent exchange, he understood that each person was equal, deserving, and worthy. After everyone was served, a contented silence fell over the makeshift food kitchen. On this cold weeknight, with quiet munching noises and muffled voices, a shared moment of peace and contentment was palpable.

The evening left an indelible impression on the young student. He hadn't anticipated feeling so uplifted by the simple task of giving to others without personal gain. "That felt really good, helping people tonight. I feel happy," he said thoughtfully; but walking back home quietly, Trevor also noticed the negative voice of scarcity thinking inside him: *I'm afraid I might end up on the street, homeless and unloved.* In the weeks following his evening at the street kitchen, he worked with these feelings of scarcity by discussing issues of poverty with his friends and family. The kind smiles he received that night from strangers had left their imprint.

Our biologies are linked. How much abundance and kindness we practice affects not only our own emotional well-being but that of others. A study found that people who engaged in intentional positive activities such as being grateful, being mindful, and being optimistic showed increased happiness (Sin & Lyubomirsky, 2009). One happiness researcher demonstrated that happy people make conscious efforts to engage in optimistic thinking and actions (Lyubomirsky, 2007). When we have a sense of fullness, we are more able and willing to benefit others.

Additionally, when we act kindly or abundantly toward another, our whole body benefits. Try this right now: Make a frowning and depressed face, collapse your posture, and notice what happens with your mood. Draw the corners of your mouth down slightly, contract your eyebrows toward each other, and collapse your chest in and downward as if you had a giant boulder sitting on top of your heart. Feel the weight and the downward pull of this posture. In less than two minutes, do you notice feeling a little blue? Now relax your muscles, soften your facial expression, and look more softly around you. What do you notice? A relaxed body creates an open heart: Your attitude brightens and your whole demeanor changes. Trevor had such an experience while serving food at the shelter. His body relaxed, and he sensed that being with the homeless was no threat to him. His mind had built up fearfulness, but his body perceived something entirely different. He was fine, and even more than fine—he was inspired and had found a purpose in helping others. In return, he felt abundance in his heart. He remembered that night for a while. Every time he talked about it with a friend, he called up this good, abundant feeling in his body.

For over twenty-five years, I have witnessed that when clients shift their body and mind, their mood follows. Assuming a happy and relaxed stance or initiating a more upright and relaxed posture creates an inner emotional shift. It doesn't take a lot of time to shift your inner mood. You simply have to be willing to become mindful about it. This is where the mindful postures we discussed under Key 2 can help. When you set up the most optimal conditions in your body posture and attitude, happiness will follow. In the same way, your physical body changes when you are generous and kind, and its felt sense is infectious for others when they know you feel good about your actions. You can initiate happiness in others and uplift your immediate environment. Naturally, this translates into direct health benefits. Your heart rate slows, and you boost your immune system.

Trevor's service experience inspired positive feelings, and in his next school project, he focused on concrete solutions for helping low-income families with new inventions he thought would be helpful. His direct experience with his own kindness and seeing that there were few barriers between him and those less fortunate inspired the beginnings of activism and care for others. When you practice mindfulness, you are that activist. You are taking an active role in changing your brain and body from the inside out. You are training your kindness muscle for yourself and others. You are developing new neural networks in your brain, and your changing brain chemistry will form new perceptions, resolve, and action. After, you are not the same. You are deciding to direct your attention and actions toward openness in your life. You are actively engaging your inner critic and are no longer trapped by past resentments and fear. It doesn't mean you won't have negative feelings anymore. But your changed physicality equips you to better handle stress and reconsider upsets as hurdles rather than endpoints.

The small acts of kindness that come with an abundance way of thinking have an impact, and there is a literal, biological reward for doing the right thing because the "feel-good" sensations translate into the release of endorphins into the body. The experience of endorphins is one where we feel connected and happy and want to reach out to others. Peace and bliss can arise, and with that a decrease in any messages of pain. In a study at York University (Mongrain, 2011), researchers wanted to know what effect daily kindness would have. The seven hundred participants noticed that by acting compassionately toward others on a daily basis, their own emotional well-being increased. They sustained the benefits for at least six months, as they reported an increase in their own self-esteem and happiness (as compared to the control group). A secondary benefit was kinder self-perception. As they practiced kindness toward others, they became kinder toward themselves.

Opening the Heart

Get literal for a moment: Imagine a giant jar of honey overflowing at the rim. The rich, sweet, amber liquid spills over. Imagine that you are this jar of honey. Your warmth and generosity overflow. Where does it want to go? Who should benefit from this plenty? Abundance feelings can arise as a sense of acceptance of who you are and where you are at in your life. You have a new apartment, small and cozy, but it is yours and you are safe. Or you feel touched by your friend's struggle with cancer and you decide to throw him a "survival" party, celebrating being alive. Abundance can be a sense of feeling emotionally secure in yourself, being content in your relationships, or being happy with the kind of work you are doing. Abundance sparkles through moments of insight such as "All is well," or "I have all I need," or "I am enough." Maybe your child acknowledges you, and even though you feel you could have done better as a parent, you pause and take it in. You are doing just fine right now.

Exercise: Heart Practice[1]

 *20–30 minutes*

This meditation focuses on becoming aware of your heart in an embodied way. The mindful heart focus serves as a reminder to the body to safely open up and see what is there. You will want to notice any resistance to feeling abundance and increasing self-kindness. Take your time. Pace yourself and see what feels right. Initially, you might not feel much or might not feel open. That's okay. Remember the focus is on present-moment awareness. If this happens, simply accept it, wait, and try again. Be patient and wait for your body and mind to settle.

1. Set the Right Frame
- Sit comfortably. Find your relaxed-alert posture.
- Scan your body for any tension and let it go as much as you can. Accept where you are as much as possible.
- Alleviate any body discomfort and settle into a relaxed outer posture. Set the intention to have an attitude of openness throughout the exercise.

2. Stay and Study
- Focus your breath awareness on your chest and heart region. First pay attention to what is there right now.
- Breathe into your heart area and connect with your body. What are the sensations here right now? Be curious and stay present.
- Stay connected with your breath as you imagine your heart in your chest. You can embellish the image if you like, but stay present in your body.

---

1. adapted from R. A. Ray, 2008a

- Imagine that there is a flower bud sitting in the middle of your heart.
- Breathe into the center of your heart and into the center of this flower bud.
- As you breathe into the heart flower, allow this image to unfold: Imagine the flower opening petal by petal as you breathe slowly and steadily.
- The flower can be anything—a rose, dahlia, lotus, daisy—but let it have abundant petals so you can witness each petal unfurling as you breathe. Let go of any wishes for this image. Accept whatever presents itself.
- Take your time. You are allowing the heart space to open through the image of the flower petals.
- If you find yourself challenged to visualize the flower, or if your flower doesn't want to open today, let that be. Next time this can be very different.
- In that case, just breathe into this heart space and stay with the experience that is there.
- If your flower opens, just follow it until it is fully open (if it's only half open, be curious about this!).
- Here are a few ways to focus: Do you feel a tenderness? Can you sense a softness in your heart? Can you detect any kindness? It may be that you become aware of an absence of a feeling that was there before. Stay with whatever your experience is and inquire. Remember that it's about your experience. These are simply directions to get you started looking.

3. Anchor and Harvest

- Let go the focus and relax your posture. Check what your inner and outer postures feel like right now.
- Reflect on the effects of this practice. See if you feel a softness or openness toward yourself. What is your experience?
- Take a moment to reflect; write in your journal if you like. It may help to take a short walk outside and see how you perceive yourself right now.
- Since this practice is about generating kindness, you may

want to pay attention to how your kindness toward yourself is showing up today. Do you notice a shift in kindness toward others?

I strongly encourage you to repeat this practice. Because you have to hold the image as well as your breath awareness, it can be easy to be distracted at first. Once you are no longer worried about the steps of the practice, you can relax into it and enter into the discovery. It's worth repeating another day and seeing if there is any difference.

Not Feeling It

Now that you have practiced opening your heart, you might also take a look at how you may be feeling any resistance. This is about making peace within. You may need to feel the hurt and grudges inside you before you can soften to the more tender parts of yourself. I call this practice "compassion in action" because you are staying right there with your own wounded or vulnerable parts; good job! You may not have been taught or given the opportunity to find or live with these softer parts of yourself. Mindfulness practice is a precious opportunity to meet yourself. When you set the intention to open your heart and practice kindness, you will no doubt encounter stories from the past or present that currently run your life. As I have stated, emotions are not to be feared but to be mindfully engaged so that you can truly understand them and see their intelligence.

After her cancer had gone into remission, Wendy had wanted to do something good for herself and signed up for a week of organized meditation, hiking, and yoga. She was looking forward to feeling well again, but she was simply not feeling it at the retreat. At mealtimes, the custom was to pause to thank the cooks for the food they had prepared for the participants. The idea sounded lovely to Wendy, but as she received her breakfast, all she could think of was how processed the food was. She became obsessed with how the bread was not whole grain, how the oatmeal was getting cold. She had worked hard during her illness and recovery to eat well and take care of her body, and now she felt unsupported in that attempt. She wasn't feeling any thoughts of abundance or softness toward anyone and was utterly absorbed in her negativity. As she became mindful in that moment, she was shocked to see her feelings of scarcity on such vivid display.

Your thinking mind, too, may show up when you want to open to abundance. You might not feel loving or kind at all. In fact, you might feel the exact opposite, with feelings of bitterness, resentment, anger, grief, and unworthiness.

What do you do in those moments? First, accept what is. There is no need to beat yourself up, and it's easy to judge during these times. Instead, have some compassion for your process. Like Wendy, you might recognize the fight against these thoughts in your head (*I should be more accepting, not so protective or pure, not so nit-picky; it's okay to eat white bread for a week . . .*). Wendy's curiosity led her to inquire about and listen compassionately to the critical words in her head. After all, that was her experience. Then she decided that it was okay to have those judgments and not beat herself up about having them. She took a breath, said to herself, "I am having a negative day," and then let it go. She practiced a mini-moment of compassion. She softened toward herself.

Throughout the book, I have emphasized how important it is to trust your experience. So again, I am asking you to trust it! However it shows up—bratty, ugly, cranky, injured—in whatever form—get curious, inquire, let it rest and settle. See if you can embrace the texture and quality of what is occurring. Relax! It's okay; some days you will be grumpy and not very kind, and other days you will notice how upbeat you are. This is what mindfulness is about—seeing clearly these rhythms and coming back to being kind to yourself and making room for all of your possibilities.

In these unloving, self-critical moments, give yourself a break. Interrupt what you've been doing. I call this "changing the channel." The mind and body need something else for a while. Change your surroundings—take a long walk or a hot bath—and you will get in touch again with who you are. Then let things settle. This is where you bridge the actual exercises of mindfulness practice with your daily life by reflecting on your thoughts, or how you are with your pet, or how you interact with a colleague at work. A key to practicing mindfulness is to become more understanding and compassionate about who you are. See if you can make room for the "inelegant" parts of you. At the meditation retreat, when Wendy understood she could accept her not-so-attractive parts, she relaxed and became more authentic and present.

The Compassion Connection

Once you open to the abundance of possibilities that come with being present to all of your experiences, you can also connect compassionately with others. The word *compassion* in Greek literally means "being moved in the guts." The Christian monk Thomas Merton taught that this value arises from a sense of the interconnectedness of all things (Johanson, 2006). When you are moved deeply in your "guts," you resonate in your body with another. You feel, sense, and participate in their experience, literally and viscerally. This is an important aspect of being mindful of others. Although you may have a tendency to jump out of thinking about another, you can come to understand the reality of the other person and begin to care. An empathic connection is vital to caring for others and developing your compassion. You are moved to action by this gut feeling.

I once saw a three-year-old boy's expression turn to sadness as he watched another child snatch a sand shovel out of his friend's hand. He walked over to his friend as she began to cry. He stiffly held up his own blue shovel, gesturing for her to take it. Her spontaneous outburst of tears had made him pause and act immediately and empathetically He wanted her to feel better, even if that meant he had to give up his beloved blue shovel. The girl looked at the ground, but the boy steadily held up the shovel, inviting her to take it. She hesitated, and her tears stopped. Gently, she grasped the handle. The boy began to dig in the sand with his hands and the girl joined with her new blue shovel. This compassionate exchange elicited tender feelings in my heart. The toddlers' direct, intense, yet nonverbal dialogue impacted me as I stood 6 feet away.

Studies of children's empathy levels reveal a strong correlation between parents' modeling of positive expressions such as gratitude, positive emotions, and praise and an increased level of empathy in their children (Eisenberg, Valiente, & Losoya, 2004). The child who is seen, emotionally received, and encouraged is free to be more empathic and compassionate. Directly experiencing empathy may embolden us to take emotional risks and feel confident to handle possible judgments. In contrast, children exposed to negative feelings in the home are more likely to be avoidant and self-protective (El-Sheikh, 2005). Another study showed that when meditators in MRI machines heard distressing sounds during their meditation, their brain's empathic circuitry responded (Lutz, Slagter, Dunne, & Davidson, 2008). Research reveals that increased empathy is directly linked to more social interactions and richer meaning and satisfaction in life (Grühn & Labouvie-Vief, 2008).

Choosing to be compassionate is not so different from choosing an abundance perspective. Most young children demonstrate natural empathy for others. Their choice is direct and immediate. As illustrated by the shovel story, where the boy was moved right away to respond empathically, children resonate with another's distress. As children grow and develop, the thinking parts of their brains, including those that make decisions about how to respond to someone's pain, become more measured. The empathy can be just as immediate, but the decision to respond becomes more constrained by social norms. For us older humans, the profound wish that we or someone else were free from suffering allows us a way to see and be *with* our pain or theirs. Yes, the pain is still there, but we can focus our attention on what is good and kind. We can learn to identify less with suffering and turn our attention to realizing a deep sense of connection with others who are in similar circumstances.

The Buddhist monk Thich Nat Hanh has talked about the many refugees who fled Vietnam during and after the war. He uses one particular story to illustrate that we are all in some "life-boat" at some point in our lives. He described how "when the crowded Vietnamese refugee boats met with storms or pirates, if everyone panicked, all would be lost. But if even one person on the boat remained calm and centered, it was enough. It showed the way for everyone to survive" (Hanh, 2005). This story resounded with me when I later met Dung, a thirty-something Vietnamese woman, who had experienced severe trauma. Dung had survived a horrible journey from Vietnam to the United States as a refugee on a boat. She had also suffered abuse as a child at the hands of a mother living with her own PTSD. The young woman's health had been gravely affected: Dung suffered from a damaged heart, which was worsening each day. She would pass out unexpectedly and was hospitalized multiple times as a result.

Yet her way of being in the world was different from that of others I had known who had suffered severe trauma. Dung had a gentleness and kindness in her that was awe-inspiring. Despite all her trauma, she remained whole by having compassion for herself and toward others. She so easily could have adopted a scarcity perspective, given the severity of her hardship. But instead, she found joy in sitting with other people's stories. She consciously chose abundance and practiced it in concrete ways. Her cheerful way of being was genuine despite how her body regularly sent her into crippling heart seizures, leaving her stranded on concrete sidewalks at the mercy of strangers. This was a condition that worsened as she grew faint and gravely ill, but she maintained a deep, calm compassion and kindness toward herself. It was as if she had seen the depths of despair and nothing could frighten her.

We are wired for survival, but we are also wired for connection. When we feel compassion toward others, our bodies respond directly. A previously agitated heart rate drops and impulses to reach out and soothe another arise. Compassion is a biologically based emotion rooted in our mammalian brain (Keltner, 2009). We have a deep human need to share and protect vulnerable offspring, but we also resonate with the emotions of others. By getting close to another human, we turn on our hormone oxytocin, which triggers feelings of warmth, trust, and connection. Oxytocin is crucial in the bonding between mother and baby and becomes the "love-glue template" of our early relationships. When we smile, have loving eye contact, or track friendly gestures, our bodies produce more oxytocin, and we feel received and cared for. We feel touched by hearing someone's story; as we release an empathetic sigh, calmness and comfort arise. We feel present and more embodied. In that moment, the vagus nerve that prepares us for fight-or-flight survival is serving us in the opposite direction by assisting us in self-soothing, reassurance, and bonding and connection. The vagus nerve gives our anxious heart rate a break, slowing us down and making us more emotionally and socially available (Carter et al., 2005). This moment of compassion motivates our bodies to be soft and kind, providing a biological inspiration to be helpful to others.

Not surprisingly, just like mindfulness, being compassionate has health benefits. It helps with stress release and gives us a happier outlook on life. Even short periods of exposure to compassion meditation, or touching into our own inner sense of abundance, decreases arousal levels in the amygdala, which is the part of the brain responsible for stress level management (Goleman 2003). According to many experts, compassion can be further developed with consistent mindfulness training (Gilbert, 2009; Weibel, 2007). Practicing compassion for others also increases self-compassion and builds life satisfaction. It reduces stress, burnout, depression, and anxiety. Research shows that compassion reduces emotional stress responses and boosts immune and neuroendocrine responses (Steptoe, Hamer, & Chida, 2007). Brain research indicates that when we feel others' emotions, it alters the neural pathways that are connected with empathy (Lutz et al., 2008). Another study found that when subjects felt compassionate love, they became more connected socially, showed greater levels of empathy, and were more motivated to be helpful (Sprecher & Fehr, 2005, 2006). I consider this kind of connection a deep wellspring of our minds and bodies. Remember the jar of honey with its overflowing sweetness? Social connection, empathy for others, and being helpful and compassionate toward yourself *are* the honey. Your jar has simply expanded and become bigger to include more than what you thought it could hold.

The feelings of softness, kindness, abundance, and compassion are inextricably linked and grow stronger the more they are felt or expressed. Dung's positive outlook on life was deeply inspiring to me as a fellow human. It wasn't just the facts of her story, but the way she embodied her abundance so authentically that it spilled, like honey, into those who surrounded her. Her kindness and exuberance were contagious and made me feel happy every time I spoke with her. I noticed that my heart opened not only toward her but toward others, as I would feel softer and be inspired to be generous. Our compassionate hearts are linked in this way. Dung's abundant compassion was infectious; she made me want to do better with others.

A study done on subjects who were practicing loving-kindness found that they showed an increased capacity for self-compassion as well as compassion toward others (Weibel, 2007). You can resonate with a friend's pain as if it is your own, but the flip side is that when you feel compassion for others, you can intimately feel not just pain but joy as well. This is what I have seen year after year in my practice with clients: the ability to face suffering fearlessly and with kindness is the magic ingredient for transforming suffering. A willingness to face pain with kindness and without judgment helps you to find acceptance and, ultimately, let the pain go or move it along. In the process, a larger understanding of your suffering occurs, and a door to profound insights and joy is unlocked. Despite her obvious suffering, Dung was brave in meeting her life as it unfolded, and her abundant, joyful attitude eased her pain. She applied herself mindfully to her illness and the people around her. She shared the joy she was experiencing with others in an inspiring way.

Recall Wendy, the client from Key 6 and earlier in this chapter, who survived cancer and faced her unresolved grief. She was willing to face what was hidden and scary at the time, and her stuck place became a gift in disguise. You, too, may not fully understand this gift at the dark times in your life, but in hindsight it will become clear. The obstacles of loss and pain can create an emotional place of no escape, but you can choose to open to this tight squeeze by softening in your body and mind. You might think you have no way out, and you may be consumed by the pain. Or you can open to the possibilities not yet known by breathing quietly and taking refuge in the interior of your mind and body. As you have learned from the stories in this book, it's possible to open to what is, no matter what. That willingness to see, feel, and become aware is mindfulness in action and brings you back to the abundance that can be found in your life experience, whatever it is. If you can do this, then you can live without limiting yourself by scarcity thinking.

Wendy blossomed after her ordeal. She went on to follow her passion in music, healed long-standing rifts with family members, and best of all, decided she was going to live fearlessly. As a result, during her meditation retreat, she found she could confront her harsh inner critic and accept her feelings as an intelligent expression of who she was in that moment. That freed up her awareness to perceive what was actually good and working in her life.

Try this:

Consider the connections in your life—human, animal, or aspects of the natural world. Are there communities you are currently part of or have been connected to in the past? Take a moment to appreciate the gifts of these connections. Can you extend a moment of gratitude to the beings you have met? Practice a moment of wishing them well, even the ones that have been challenging or the ones you are no longer in active contact with. What happens?

An Abundant Presence

How do you develop a way of being that is truly compassionate and abundant? All along you have been getting ready for this practice with the 8 Keys. As you stop and get curious, feel and sense your body's rhythms, and acknowledge your emotions and the places that are hard to face, and as you soften toward others and listen with an open heart, you are choosing to practice abundance, mindfulness, and compassion. You are realigning your heart to what has meaning, not in grand gestures but in consistent acts of kindness toward yourself and others.

When asked during an interview what was essential to acting as well as life, actor Hugh Jackman gave this advice: "Don't be afraid to fall on your face and make a fool of yourself. It's about presence—have a free breath and emotions." This presence, a quality of wakeful attention to the breath, to the body, to the moment, is a gift you can feel when you are connected to your authentic self, no matter your state. Your body, your senses, and your energy flow in tandem with the world around you. You redefine your "self" as part of an interconnected whole (Siegel, 2010). You are here and you know that you are here, nowhere else. You and your abundant presence find complete alignment with the present moment. Practicing mindfulness on a regular basis becomes a set of training wheels for developing more presence and wakefulness in your life. Do you have the courage to bring this into your life on a daily basis? What would that look like?

Everyday Mindfulness Tip

When you go to bed, reflect on the day you had. Go through the details of who you talked to and what you did. Pick one or two moments of this day that you are grateful for. Take a breath and state this aloud. For example, you could say, "I am grateful for my body today" or "I felt at ease in the meeting at the office today. I was able to breathe during my presentation even though I was scared." Or even more simply, you could be grateful for the life you feel in your body: "I feel and sense my breath and am grateful to be alive. I am thankful to my stomach and digestive system for breaking down the food I ate today and nourishing all of my cells." If you want to include another thought, you might say: "I am grateful for the kindness of my family and friends." Then focus on your out-breath; visualize the exhale being soft and dissolving and let the day go. Remember to hold in the back of your mind an attitude of abundance.

MINDFULNESS FOR THE ROAD

Kindness gives birth to kindness. —SOPHOCLES

Mindfulness for the Road

Practicing mindfulness is the path to becoming more accepting of yourself and others. You meet yourself in ways that are intimate and direct. The teachings in this book guide you to embrace your emotions, trust your body, and slow down so you can feel and hear what is happening on a deeper level inside and listen to the deeper truths of who you are and what you care about. It's that simple. You simply need to learn to get out of your own way and have the courage to listen to what is true and right, and to act from this place of inner alignment. The 8 Keys are about listening and living with an awake and kind heart.

There are opportunities for mindfulness everywhere. As you have been learning through the stories in the book, mindfulness can often arise when least expected. Of course, the more you consciously practice "grooving" that mindfulness muscle the more you will recognize and want to experience these moments. A sense of confidence will arise. You will experience more and more moments that you can meet head on without fear.

Create opportunities for mindfulness in your daily life. There is the official, daily sitting down and making room for practice. These "training wheels" are crucial. Without them, you can become complacent and not take seriously that mindfulness needs cultivation. You might think that you can squeeze in mindfulness here and there, but the obstacles are not far away. Laziness might take over and you will find yourself undisciplined. Make daily or at least weekly room for your mindfulness time. If you truly want to bring the benefits of mindfulness into your life, you need to make space for it. Create new habits that support this effort. You might practice in the morning or during your lunch break or when the house is quiet at night. Choose a time and stick to it. That way you can notice how you avoid it, get bored, or check out. You can also see how you are reaping the benefits and feel the changes that are truly taking shape.

Outside of daily or weekly practice, look for opportunities during your everyday life. Do you find yourself waiting in the dentist's office? Instead of grabbing your PDA and checking your email, why not take this moment of space and sit with it? Are you hanging out at your child's baseball game? Take a moment as you watch on the sidelines. Breathe and notice your body. A great time to practice Sky meditation (p. 152) is when you see the vast sky above you. Snippets of time such as these are opportunities to notice and be curious. Check in with the temptation to "fill space." In this device- and stimulus-driven world, it's easy to fill space by consuming information, which will bring you out of direct experience with yourself and the world around you. Get radical. Make a conscious choice to come into relationship with your direct experience.

Go even further and broaden your sphere. Give a moment of mindfulness to someone. Try giving a loving thought to someone in need. Dedicate your next meditation to someone who is depressed or down. Share you mindfulness with others. Be generous when you practice and take the time to calm your mind. Wish that for someone else. Stop rushing around and simply pause to listen to someone's story. Give them the gift of a few genuine moments of your undivided attention. Put down the phone and look at your child's face, cherishing his or her account of the day. When you find yourself speeding up, slow down. There is always a minute to pause and wait.

When you are experiencing stress or hardship, step out, walk, take a moment away, reflect, and tend to your body-mind. Tune in to your breath, body, and mind, and notice where you are. Honor your feelings, sensations, and moods. Let them be and cultivate a kind attitude toward yourself. It will become second nature if you continue to practice. Many mindfulness studies have proven that even after six weeks of regular mindfulness, the brain and body change. Your mood lifts, your mind calms, and you gain tools to regulate emotional roller coasters. The trick is to stay with it and not be derailed by the obstacles. Return to previous chapters and do the exercises that feel appropriate to this particular moment in your journey. Mindful awareness needs to be cultivated and learned, but it is a practice that will pay off.

There will always be difficulties. You will encounter emotional places where you go to sleep. You will make mistakes, hold on to old habits, and resist change. But you can come back to yourself again and again. This is what developing a mindfulness practice is all about: the willingness to start again, each time fresh and with open attitude. It's not about meeting a goal but about creating a toolkit for living your life with heart and meaning. It's about finding an inner compass that you can rely on wherever you go. Becoming mindful is to become your own best friend. You can trust your experience, you can trust your body, and with that you can learn to trust your mind.

Where Do I Go Next?

My hope is that this book has inspired you to develop your own mindfulness practice. It is very beneficial to join others who enjoy practicing mindfulness, and we are fortunate to live in a time where you can join sitting groups, go on a longer meditation retreat, listen to recordings, or read further in print or online. I encourage you to repeat the exercises in the book as often as you wish. Maybe there were favorites you liked? Maybe you avoided others? Take a look and consider trying out the ones you avoided.

I urge you to come up with a daily routine. Practice short exercises such as "Simple Breath Awareness" (p. 40) or "Brain, Heart,

Belly Sequence" (p. 55) and make them part of your regular routine. Over time, this will become second nature to you, and you will find it easier to include the other practices. There is no set recipe here. It's about you tuning in to what works for your stage of your life and your circumstances. The key is your own motivation. When you notice yourself slacking off, you might pick up the chapter on emotions (Key 5) and discover there were aspects you did not address. See if you can return to the chapters as you find that they fit your life. They are meant to inspire you in your own mindfulness practice.

Remember the baseline measurement you took of your life under Key 1 (p. 15)? Try returning to this exercise and looking at where you are now. What has changed for you, now that you've reached the end of this book? Recall that a baseline is a reference point for who you are and what you have in any given moment. It's a dot on your life's map or trajectory. The idea is to notice what is present right now. At this time, consider what works in your life and what doesn't work.

Consider sitting with others by finding a meditation group or teacher. Perform acts of kindness in your life, and branch out. When you touch important milestones in your mindfulness practice, write them down, share them, and then find opportunities to implement them in your life. Maybe you had a very tender experience in your meditation today and you decide that you will have a positive attitude because of it. See what smiles come your way as you impact your own life in this way.

Although mindfulness has become an accepted part of popular culture, it is not a fad. It's a way of bettering your life. It's *for* you. And it's *up* to you. The more you invest in your mental health, the more you will reap the benefits of a clear, calm, and stable mind. Practice, practice, practice, both on your cushion and in your life. Life's challenges are easier to ride when you have a cool head and a kind heart.

References

Aiken, G. A. (2006). The potential effect of mindfulness meditation on the cultivation of empathy in psychotherapy: A qualitative inquiry. *Dissertation Abstracts International, Section B: Sciences and Engineering, 67,* 2212.

Ainley, V., & Tsakiris, M. (2013). Body Conscious? Interoceptive Awareness, Measureed by Heartbeat Perception, is Negatively Correlated with Self-Objectification. *PLOS ONE* 8 (2):e55568.doi.10.1371/journal.pone.0055568.

Baer, R. A., Lykins, E. L. B., & Peters, J. R. (2012). Mindfulness and self-compassion as predictors of psychological wellbeing in long-term meditators and matched nonmeditators. *Journal of Positive Psychology, 7*(3), 230–238.

Balaji, P. A., Varne, S. R., & Sadat, A. S. (2012). Physiological effects of yogic practices and transcendental meditation in health and disease. *North American Journal of Medical Sciences, 4*(10), 442–448.

Beddoe, A. E., & Murphy, S. O. (2004). Does mindfulness decrease stress and foster empathy among nursing students? *Journal of Nursing Education.* 43(7). 305-312.

Bernardi, L., Sleight, P., Bandinelli, G., Fattorini, L., Wdowczyc-Szulc, J., & Lagi, A. (2001). Effect of rosary prayer and yoga mantras on autonomic cardiovascular rhythms: Comparative study. *BMJ, 323,* 1446–1449.

Bodhi, B. (2000). *The connected discourses of the Buddha: A translation of the Samyutta Nikaya.* Boston, MA: Wisdom.

Bowen, S., Witkiewitz, K., Dillworth, T. M., Chawla, N., Simpson, T. L., Ostafin, B. D., . . . Marlatt, G. A. (2006). Mindfulness meditation and substance use in an incarcerated population. *Psychology of Addictive Behaviors, 20,* 343–347.

Bowen, S., Witkiewitz, K., Dillworth, T. M., & Marlatt, G. A. (2007). The role of thought suppression in the relationship between mindfulness meditation and alcohol use. *Addictive Behaviors, 32,* 2324–2328.

Breines, J. G., & Chen, S. (2013). Activating the inner caregiver: The role of support-giving schemas in increasing state self-compassion. *Journal of Experimental Social Psychology, 49*(1), 58–64.

Briñol, P., Petty, R. E., & Wagner, B. (2009). Body posture effects on self-evaluation: A self-validation approach. *European Journal of Social Psychology, 39,* 1053–1064.

Brown, B. (2010). *The gifts of imperfection: Let go of who you think you are supposed to be and embrace who you are.* Center City, MN: Hazelden.

Brown, K. W., Ryan, R. M., & Creswell, J. D. (2007). Addressing fundamental questions about mindfulness. *Psychological Inquiry, 18,* 272–281.

Brown, S. (2010). *Play. How it shapes the brain, opens the imagination, and invigorates the soul.* New York: Avery Trade.

Bruckstein, D. C. (1999). Effects of acceptance-based and cognitive behavioral interventions on chronic pain management. *Dissertation Abstracts International: Section B: The Sciences & Engineering, 60*(1-B), p. 0359.

Cacioppo, J. T., Ito, T. A., Larsen, J. T., & Smith K. (1998). Negative information weighs more heavily on the brain: The negativity bias in evaluative categorizations. *Journal of Personality and Social Psychology, 75*(4), 887–900.

Capurso, V., Fabbro, F., & Crescentini, C. (2013). Mindful creativity: The influence of mindfulness meditation on creative thinking. *Frontiers in Psychology, 4,* 1020.

Carney, D., Cuddy, A., & Yap, A. J. (2010). Power posing: Brief nonverbal displays affect neuroendocrine levels and risk tolerance. *Psychological Science, 21*(10), 133–168.

Carter, C. S., Ahnert L., Grossmann, K., Hardy, S. B., Lamb, M., Porges, S. W., & Sachser, N. (Eds.) (2005). *Attachment and bonding: A new synthesis.* Cambridge, MA: MIT Press.

Cuddy, A. J. C., Kohut, M., & Neffiger, J. (2013). Connect, Then Lead. Trust is the conduit of influence. *Harvard Business Review 91,* nos 7/8:5–61.

Damasio, A. (1994). *Descartes' error: Emotion, reason and the human brain.* New York: Grosset/Putnam.

Davis, J. M., Fleming, M. F., Bonus, K. A., & Baker, T. B. (2007). A pilot study on mindfulness based stress reduction for smokers. *British Medical Journal Complementary and Alternative Medicine, 7,* 2.

Desbordes, G., Barbieri, R., Citi, L., Lazar, S., Negi, L. T., Raison, C., & Schwartz, E. L. (2012). Longitudinal effects of two types of mediation training on brain responses to emotional stimuli in an ordiary, non-meditative state. *Human Neuroscience, 1*(6), 292.

Easterlin, B. L., & Cardena, E. (1999). Cognitive and emotional differences between short- and long-term vipassana meditators. *Imagination, Cognition, and Personality, 18,* 69–81.

Eisenberg, N., Valiente, C., & Losoya, S. (2004). Prediction of children's empathy-related responding from their effortful control and parents' expressivity. *Developmental Psychology, 40*(6), 911–926.

El-Sheikh, M. (2005). The role of emotional responses and physiological reactivity in the marital conflict-child functioning link. *Journal of Child Psychology and Psychiatry, 46*(11), 1191–1199. doi: 10.1111 /j.1469-7610.2005.01418.x

Farb, N. A. S., & Anderson, A. K. (2010). Minding one's emotions: Mindfulness training alters the neural expression of sadness. *Emotion, 10*(1), 25–33.

Follette, V. M., & Vijay, A. (2009). Mindfulness for trauma and post-traumatic stress disorder. In F. Didonna (Ed.), *Clinical handbook of mindfulness* (pp. 299–317). New York: Springer Science + Business Media.

Germer, C. K., & Neff, K. D. (2013). Self-compassion in clinical practice. *Journal of Clinical Psychology, 69*(8), 856–867.

Gilbert, P. (2009). *The compassionate mind: A new approach to life's challenges.* Constable-Robinson.

Goleman, D. (2003). *Destructive emotions and how we can overcome them: A dialogue with the Dalai Lama.* London, UK: Bantam.

Grühn, D. R. K., & Labouvie-Vief, G. (2008). Empathy across the adult lifespan: Longitudinal and experience-sampling findings. *Emotion, 8*(8), 753–765. Retrieved from http://www.ncbi.nlm.nih.gov/pmc/ articles/PMC2669929/

Hanson, R. (2009). *Buddha's brain. The practical neuroscience of happiness, love and wisdom.* Oakland, CA: New Harbinger.

Hanh, T. N. (2005). *Being peace* (2nd ed.). Parallax Press.

Hebb, D. (1949). *The organization of behavior.* New York: Wiley & Sons.

Hölzel B. K. Carmody, J., & Vangel, M. (2011). Mindfulness practice leads to increases in regional brain gray matter density. *Psychiatry Research: Neuroimaging, 191*(1), 36–43

Jha, A. P., Krompinger, J., & Baime, M. J. (2007). Mindfulness training modifies subsystems of attention. *Cognitive, Affective, and Behavioral Neuroscience, 7,* 109–119.

Jha, A. P., & van Vugt, M. K. (2011). Investigating the impact of mindfulness meditation training on working memory: A mathematical modeling approach. *Cognitive, Affective, and Behavioral Neuroscience, 11,* 344–353. doi: 10.3758/s13415-011-0048-8

Johanson, G. J. (2006). A survey of the use of mindfulness in psychotherapy. *Annals of American Psychotherapy Association, 9*(2), 15–24.

Johnson, W. (1996). *The posture of meditation: A practical manual for mediators of all traditions.* Boston, MA: Shambhala.

Kabat-Zinn, J., Massion, A. O., Kristeller, J., Peterson, L. G., Fletcher, K., Pbert, L., Linderking, W., & Santorelli, S. F. (1992). Effectiveness of a meditation-based stress reduction program in the treatment of anxiety disorder. *American Journal Psychiatry, 149,* 936–943.

Keltner, D. (2009). *Born to be good: The science of a meaningful life* (1st ed.). New York: W. W. Norton.

Kilpatrick, L. A., Suyenobu, B. Y., Smith, S. R., Bueller, J. A., Goodman, T., . . . Naliboff, B. D. (2011). Impact of mindfulness-based stress reduction training on intrinsic brain connectivity. *Neuroimage, 56*(1), 290–298.

King, A. P., Erickson, T. M., Giardino, N. D., Favorite, T., Rauch, S. A., Robinson, E., Kulkarni, M., Liberzon, I. (2013). A pilot study of group mindfulness-based cognitive therapy (MBCT) for combat veterans with Postraumatic Stress Disorder (PTSD). *Depression and Anxiety, 20*(7), 638–645.

Lazar, S. W., Kerr, C. E., Wasserman, R. H., Greve, D. N., Treadway, M. T., . . . Quinn, B. (2005). Meditation experience is associated with increased cortical thickness. *NeuroReport , 16*(17), 1893–1897. doi: 10.1097/01.wnr.0000186598.66243.19

Levine, P. (2010). *In an unspoken voice: How the body releases trauma and restores goodness.* Berkeley, CA: North Atlantic Books.

Litchfield, P. M. A. (2003) Brief overview of the chemistry of respiration and the breathing heart wave. *California Biofeedback, 19*(1).

Litchfield, P. M. (2006). Good breathing, bad breathing: Breathing is behavior, a unique behavior that regulates body chemistry, pH. Retrieved March 15, 2014, from http://www.scribd.com/doc/40537212 /Good-Breathing-Bad-Breathing

Litman, R. (2012). *Interview by M. Mischke-Reeds: The breathable body.* Retrieved 2012 from http://thebreathablebody.com

Lutz, A., Slagter, H. A., Dunne, J. D., & Davidson, R. J. (2008). Attention regulation and monitoring in meditation. *Trends in Cognitive Sciences, 12,* 163–169. doi:10.1016/j.tics.2008.01.005

Lyubomirsky, S. (2007). *The how of happiness: A new approach to getting the life you want.* New York: Penguin Books.

McKim, R. D. (2008). Rumination as a mediator of the effects of mind-

fulness: Mindfulness-based stress reduction (MNSR) with a hetero-
geneous community sample experiencing anxiety, depression, and/
or chronic pain. *Dissertation Abstracts International: Section B: The
Sciences and Engineering, 68,* 7673.

Modinos, G., Ormel, J., & Aleman, A. S. (2010). Individual differences
in dispositional mindfulness and brain activity involved in reap-
praisal of emotion. *Social Cognitive Affective Neuroscience Advance
Access.* doi: 10.1093/scan/nsq006

Newberg, A. (2010). *How God changes your brain: Breakthrough findings
from a leading neuroscientist.* New York: Ballantine Books.

Perry, B. D. (2004). Maltreatment and the developing child: How early
childhood experience shapes child and culture. Retrieved 2013 from
childtrauma.org

Pert, C. (2010). *Molecules of emotion: The Science behind mind-body
medicine.* New York: Scribner.

Porges, S. (2011). *The polyvagal theory: Neurophysiological foundations
of emotions, attachment, communication, and self-regulation.* New
York: W. W. Norton.

Ray, R. A. (2008a). *Touching enlightenment: Finding realization in the
body.* Boulder, CO: Sounds True.

Ray, R. A. (2008b). *Your breathing body, Volumes 1 and 2.* [Audio CD]
Boulder, CO: Sounds True.

Ray, R. A. (2012). Learn to Meditate: Awakening the Heart. Retrieved
September 15, 2014, from http://www.dharmaocean.org/meditation/
learn-to-meditate/learn-to-meditate-awakening-the-heart/.

Schore, A., & Bradshaw, G. A. (2006). How elephants are opening doors:
Developmental neuroethology: Attachment and social context.
Ethology, 113, 426–436. doi: 10.1111/j.1439-0310.2007.01333.

Segal, Z. V., Williams, J. M. G., & Teasdale, J. D. (2002). *Mindfulness-
based cognitive therapy for depression: A new approach to preventing
relapse.* New York: Guilford Press.

Shapiro, S. L., Schwartz, G. E., & Bonner, G. (1998). Effects of
mindfulness-based stress reduction on medical and premedical students. *Journal of Behavioral Medicine, 21,* 581–599. doi:10.1023/A:
1018700829825

Siegel, D. (2010). *Mindsight: The new science of personal transformation.*
New York: Bantam Books.

Siegel, D. (2013). *Brainstorm: The power and purpose of the teenage
brain.* New York: Penguin.

Sin, N. L., & Lyubomirsky, S. (2009). Enhancing well-being and allevi-
ating depressive symptoms with positive psychology interventions: a

practice-friendly meta-analysis. *Journal of Clinical Psychology, 65*(5), 467–487.

Singh, N. N., Lancioni, G. E., Winton, A. S. W., Fisher, B. C., Wahler, R. G., McAleavey, K., . . . Sabaawi, M. (2006). Mindful parenting decreases aggression, noncompliance, and self-injury in children with autism. *Journal of Emotional and Behavioral Disorders, 14*(3), 169–177.

Sprecher, S., & Fehr, B. (2005). Compassionate love for close others and humanity. *Journal of Social and Personal Relationships, 22,* 629–651.

Sprecher, S., & Fehr, B. (2006). Enhancement of mood and self-esteem as a result of giving and receiving compassionate love. *Current Research in Social Psychology, 11,* 227–242.

Steptoe, A., Hamer, M., & Chida, Y. (2007). The effect of acute psychological stress on circulating inflammatory factors in humans: A review and meta-analysis. *Brain, Behavior, and Immunity, 21*(7), 901–912.

Strack, F., Martin, L. L., & Stepper, S. (1988). Inhibiting and facilitating conditions of the human smile: A nonobtrusive test of the facial feedback hypothesis. *Journal of Personality and Social Psychology, 54,* 768–777.

Streeter, C. C., Gerbarg, P. L., Saper, R. B., Ciraulo, D. A., & Brown, R. P. (2012). Effects of yoga on the autonomic nervous system, gamma-aminobutyric-acid, and allostasis in epilepsy, depression, and post-traumatic stress disorder. *Medical Hypotheses, 78*(5), 571–579.

Saraswati, S. M., & Saraswati, S. S. (2000). *The hatha yoga pradipka.* Yoga Publication Trust.

Tanga, Y. Y., Maa, Y., Fana, Y., Fenga, H., Wanga, J., Fenga, S., . . . Fanc, M. (2009). *Central and autonomic nervous system interaction is altered by short-term meditation.* Retrieved March 16, 2014, from http://www.pnas.org/content/106/22/8865.abstract

Taylor Bolte, J. (2008). *My stroke of insight: A brain scientist's personal journey.* New York: Viking Adult.

Trungpa, C. (2009). *Smile at fear: Awakening the true heart of bravery.* Boston, MA: Shambhala.

Trungpa, C. (2010). *Training the mind and cultivating loving-kindness.* Boston, MA: Shambhala.

Toneatto, T., & Nguyen, L. (2007). Does mindfulness meditation improve anxiety and mood symptoms? A review of the controlled research. *Canadian Journal of Psychiatry, 52,* 260–266.

U.S. Department of Veterans Affairs. (n.d.). *PTSD: National Center for PTSD.* Retrieved March 14, 2014 from http://www.ptsd.va.gov

Wang, S. J. (2007). Mindfulness meditation: Its personal and professional impact on psychotherapists. *Dissertation Abstracts International, Section B: Science and Engineering, 67,* 4122.

Weibel, D. T. (2007). *A loving-kindness intervention: Boosting compassion for self and others.* Doctoral dissertation, Ohio University. Retrieved from http://ezproxy.lib.ucf.edu/login?url= http://search.proquest.com/docview/304817410?accountid=10003

Zeidan, F., Martucci, K. T., Kraft, R. A., Gordon, N. S., McHaffie, J. G., & Coghill, R. C. (2011). Brain mechanisms supporting the modulation of pain by mindfulness meditation. *Journal of Neuroscience, 31*(14), 5540–5548.

Resources

About the Author's Teachings and Trainings
Teaching and Consulting: www.mindingthepresent.com
Psychotherapy Practice: www.somaticinquiry.com
Hakomi Institue of California: www.hakomica.org

Web Resources on Mindfulness and Compassion
http://greatergood.berkeley.edu
http://www.mindfulexperience.org
http://marc.ucla.edu
http://ccare.stanford.edu
http://www.soundstrue.com

Meditation Training and Retreats
Reginald A. Ray and the Dharma Ocean, www.dharmaocean.org
Center for Mindfulness, www.umassmed.edu

Mindfulnes-Based Psychotherapy Training and Therapist Directory
Hakomi Institute, www.hakomiinstitute.com
Hakomi Institute of California, www.hakomica.org

Somatic Trauma Therapy and Training
Somatic Experiencing Trauma Institute, www.traumahealing.com/
 somatic-experiencing
Somatic Trauma Therapy, www.somatictraumatherapy.com

Universities That Include Mindfulness in Their Programs
California Institute of Integral Studies, www.ciis.edu
JFK University, www.jfku.edu
Naropa University, www.naropa.edu

Index